The C Word
edited by Kate North

INDEPENDENT INNOVATIVE INTERNATIONAL

Published by Cinnamon Press
Meirion House
Glan yr afon
Tanygrisiau
Blaenau Ffestiniog
Gwynedd LL41 3SU
www.cinnamonpress.com

The right of the contributors to be identified as the authors of this
work has been asserted by them in accordance with the Copyright,
Designs and Patent Act, 1988. © 2011
ISBN 978-1-907090-50-9
British Library Cataloguing in Publication Data. A CIP record for
this book can be obtained from the British Library

Designed and typeset in Garamond by Cinnamon Press.
Cover design by Jan Fortune from original artwork 'Cardiff Buildings' by
Karen Owens © Karen Owens, agency dreamtime.

Cinnamon Press is represented by Inpress and by the Welsh Books Council
in Wales.

Printed in Poland

Acknowledgements

The production of this book would not have been possible without
the assistance of HEFCW, Cardiff School of Education, Gill Jones
and UWIC Research & Enterprise Services, Jan and her wonderful
crew at Cinnamon Press, Spencer Jordan and Meryl Hopwood for
their editorial assistance and the support of colleagues in the UWIC
Humanities department in general.

Contents

Poetry

Introduction

When putting the submissions call out for this anthology I deliberately avoided setting criteria for the contents and subject matter. I wanted the tone of the anthology to be set by the contributors, for a fairly simple reason. I was intrigued. I wanted to see what writers based in Cardiff were choosing to write about, ten years after devolution and in the wake of the huge developments and redevelopments that the city has encountered.

I was provided with an escape from Cardiff for an unexpected sexual encounter in A. Owen James' *8*, a meditation on the status of women through a re-imagining of biblical myth with L. Windridge's *Dirty Words*. Ben Jones' moving and elegant *Aelwyn* took me to the north of Wales whereas Siobhan Tumetly's touching *Blanket on the Ground* is set on the day of a funeral in Cardiff. In Emma Hutson's *Remember?* an adult narrator hallucinates and ends up in a conversation with her former teenage self, provoking both humour and poignancy and Barry Hogan takes us travelling again in *A Return To Brighton*. Liam Johnson's mixed genre *Decembruary 54th* introduces us to a world orchestrated through stream of consciousness, social media and free verse. Ashleigh Davies' poetry sparkles with lyricism whereas Danica Green's verse mixes the acerbic with wit.

As I suspected it would be, the contents of this anthology is lively, dramatic, original and diverse. Each of the authors showcased are completing or have completed a degree at the University of Wales Institute, Cardiff. It has been a real pleasure and privilege to bring together these talented voices in one publication that offers a glimpse into the creativity, diversity and dynamism that the capital affords its lucky residents.

Kate North

The C Word

Siobhan Tumelty

Blanket on the ground

It will be done with today. It's ten in the morning and I can't get my hair right. However early I get up, however prepared I plan to be, when I need to get my hair right it mocks me from the mirror. It's the worst kind of sticky hot, I'm showered but I can feel the sweat pooling at the base of my back. When I look closely to apply my foundation I see perfect beads amongst the faint hair on my upper lip. I don't know why I bother.

You can't polish a turd. That's what Jack would say, and I would never really know if he was joking as he passed behind me. If you could trust anyone to tell the truth, it would be him. He won't be there today, he doesn't do awkward. I wish I had his guts. But then he doesn't really remember her and no one's going to make him. It surprises me. There are only fifteen months between us but they make all the difference when it comes to remembering.

Peanuts, I remember peanuts. There was always a massive plastic jar of K.P. salted nuts. I've always preferred them to dry roasted, maybe that's why. I was only allowed them there- she used to give them to me one at a time and watch me eat them.

Chew chew chew chew, open your mouth, let me see. Ok. Swallow. Mum would have had a fit. She didn't leave me there often, but I loved it when she did. There was a giant fish tank with castles and deep sea divers. Bubbles spewed out of a little tube at the bottom, and I wondered if they tickled the fish. I'd leave K.P. greasy mitt marks all over the glass but she didn't mind.

It's funny, the things that stay. Inconsequential bits mainly, but you can't help what you remember. I blot my lip with tissue and little bits of white fluff stick there. *Shit.* Does it matter how I look? There are cameras at all the other milestones in life, why does nobody photograph a funeral? I head to the kitchen and pour myself a drink. Gin and juice in the morning, most breakfast-like. The order of service sits on the breakfast bar; Matthew sent one over so we could check it. She stares out at me from the front page. It's an old photo, from her house. There were none of her in the boxes and boxes at my mother's.

9

She looks how I remembered her. Smiling with a big old gob of perfect teeth, just like mine, just like Mum's. Gold strung around her neck like Christmas garlands. She had perfectly manicured nails and there was always a fag between her first and second finger. No smoking around the children though. Those were the rules. So when I went home with a burn in the back of my shell suit where she'd been pushing me on the swings, it kicked off a treat. *Swish swish swish*. There is not a child born in the mid 80s who did not love the swishing of a shell suit – I would stake my life on it.

I'm glad I wore black. I don't know if I'm in mourning but the half-arsed grey looks shit on Matthew. The sweat on his back is seeping through his shirt and he looks like he's just been for a run. Nice. Just that little bit older than me again; his memories are probably ten times what mine are. He used to walk me to the sweet shop at the end of her street for ten p. mix. Giant cola bottles and Bubbaloo. I don't think I was supposed to tell Mum about those either. I would sit cross legged in front of the T.V. and watch him play Sega, drinking pop that she used to get from the milk man.

I think of my dad in all of this. I'd always known she'd hated him. I don't think I ever saw them in the same room. It was wrong of her, the way she'd gotten back in touch. You're not supposed to shoot the messenger but what if it's to save your embarrassment, your shame? A flamboyant woman in her sixties, he'd said, wears a head scarf. Dying of cancer and all she wanted was to see her grand children, kept from her for eighteen years. That's not the kind of thing you tell a stranger in a pub. She'd gotten talking to him, a friend of a friend, and all the policemen in this city know each other – it was only a matter of time before it got back to him. Mortified. Angry. How did that make him look?

I used to ask, for a while, but I learned not to. Then I would just get excited when the car seemed to be heading in her direction- up to the last minute when we'd go somewhere else. Gradually I forgot, I suppose. I saw her once, when I was a little older. Her and Grampy Bill, who was never my Grampy, just one of her boyfriends – and quite possibly the father of one of my uncles. They were stood in the kitchen at Matthew's, but we didn't stay long.

I can feel the eyes on us, the family. We're sat at the front but we don't belong there. There's the big fat lady from next door who used to do her nails. Some other neighbours, a selection of hard looking women with Ely face lifts, a man with one arm. The coffin sits at the front draped in a Welsh flag. She'd specified, it was all planned out; we hadn't had to choose anything. From the daffs to the song as they drew around the curtain, it had all been there in her old lady hand writing. Next to the lists for cat food and fags – her send off. I used to look for that hand writing on envelopes, birthdays and Christmas. In my callous mid teens I figured she owed me at least £200 quid in present money – I hadn't done anything wrong, what kind of a Nan was she anyway?

I'd always wonder. When I got a job in Marksies one year I was convinced I'd see her. Everyone shops in Marksies. I'd be there beeping through the jumpers and she'd recognise me over the knit wear. Or maybe she wouldn't. Maybe I'd sold her a purple turtle neck and neither of us would have known. It's possible. My memories were vague enough, and I certainly wasn't five anymore.

She'd looked tiny, when I did see her. My uncle David, Matthew's dad, had sorted it in the end. They'd always stayed in touch, even though he did see her on his own. You've only got one mother, that's what he'd say. Even if she was everything they said she was. How can you be mad at someone with the frame of a 12 year old? She was propped up in a hospital bed in the front room, by the window. A complete stranger. I was no stranger to her. The walls were covered in photographs of us all as children. I stared down at my 23 year old self from frame after frame. There were still peanuts in a jar on the coffee table. My mum called her 'mam.' I'd never heard her say it before, it surprised me. She sat at the head of the bed with her tiny hand in her palm. *It's ok, mam, it's ok.*

I looked at her now. I thought of the whole lifetime that she'd had before I was born. I wasn't there, I'd never know. I'd learned in dribs and drabs as I'd got older. What had happened, who'd done what. Yet there she was, standing at the front twisting a tissue in her hands, ignoring the stares from the other side of the room.

I hadn't known what to say to her, this woman with my picture in her purse. I sat next to her and she smiled, held my hand and closed her eyes. Her hair was short and fluffy from the chemo and I wanted to touch it. I wanted to ask her a million things, I wanted to know her. She slept most of the time I was there until the nurses came in to wash her, so I left them alone. Mum and David were sat in the living room drinking tea. It was lunch time so I popped up the road to the shops for a pot noodle. She died while I was deciding between chow mein and mild curry.

I didn't cry then. I'm not crying now. I wish I could but I'd feel like a fraud. I wish that I wasn't looking at the vicar type man standing at the front leading this funeral by numbers and praying he'd hurry up. Maybe it's because of this stoicism that they asked me to do a reading. Nothing special, Corinthians, I think. She wasn't religious or anything but everybody likes to think that maybe, just maybe they're going to a better place.

So will it be with the resurrection of the dead. The body that is sown is perishable; it is raised imperishable; It is sown in dishonour, it is raised in glory; It is sown in weakness, it is raised in power; It is sown a natural body, it is raised a spiritual body.

The words come out and I look up from the pulpit. I take a second, to steady my voice. Mum is crying, David is crying, the man with one arm is crying and I don't even know who he is. There's a plain pine box behind me and in it is a little old lady. Suddenly I get it. All of a sudden I am sad, and I start to cry. I'm crying for my mum and for everything that she's been through, I'm crying for her mam and all her years on her own. I am sobbing in front of a room full of people because I can't even finish the reading for her. Matthew stands and does it for me.

I go to my mum and I hold her hand. The rest of the funeral passes in a blur until the final song. As the curtain's going around and we're making our way out a Country and Western song twangs from the speakers. It's about sneaking out in the moonlight and having sex on a blanket. It's ridiculously inappropriate, like we're leaving a barn dance. I look at my mother and she shakes her head. She remembers it from somewhere. I decide not to ask.

Ben Jones

Aelwyn

The last glowing embers fell from the diminished cigarette as Aelwyn flicked it to the ground. He used the butt of his walking stick to grind it down, extinguish it, and resumed his dialogue with the reddening sun. He often came here to this bench, my wife Pamela who loved the beach engraved into the backrest, to converse silently across the waves. And every time he wished he could stay there after the sun had fled and the white pinpricks came out and took its place, but they weren't warm and his leg hated them. He pulled out the black clamshell from his pocket, flipped it open, and squinted at the screen. Just a blur. Both hands on the wooden stick he hauled himself to his feet, muttering a Iesu Mawr and rubbing his right leg.

– Until tomorrow, or another day, Pamela, he said by way of a goodbye, and had he been wearing a hat he would have doffed it.

He lit another cigarette and took a few deep drags. Warmed by the smoke he made his way up the promenade, his stick mirroring his bad leg in its swings. Snatches of laughter caught his ear and he glanced right to the chalets, most with their doors smashed in and none of them part of the rainbow of colour that he held in his head. There should be people here, gathering their towels and dressing their children, putting away picnics. It was a Saturday. He would keep his parents here long after the rest had left, after the sand and promenade was deserted and the sea had claimed whatever feats of architecture had been forgotten. He would just stare out into the blue and grey, pointing out every boat that he saw until he was dragged into the chalets to change. A football thudded and laughs came again, and as Aelwyn passed a dead ice cream stall a group of boys, all about thirteen with cigarettes poking from their mouths, came into view. The ball rolled to his feet and cane and he pretended it hadn't.

– You gonna kick it back? The boys laughed.

His leg screamed and he ignored them, walked past. Under the bridge which a train shook and between the paintings on the tunnel walls, Aelwyn's stick clicked twice and thrice for every strike. Out in the red sun Paradise Road took up his view, but a paradise it was

13

not. It was steep, potholed and long. As if in preparation he took another huge drag of smoke, burning the white tube down to its orange feet. It collapsed under his cane as he set it down to light a virgin stick. Then he stepped forwards and time slowed, everything slowed. The still bright mountains ahead overpowered his leg, its once incessant complaints quieted. The sun coloured the blast pit of the quarry, the granite shining a deep red. He would sit on the side of those pits, watching the night creep in and relishing the cool breeze that came with it as it cooled and refreshed him, sweat and fatigue sloughing from his body. Nobody watches down from there now, the sun ignored as it falls between the sea and the sky. The granite is not gone. The *need* is. Forgotten and ignored, too high for the waves to reclaim and wash away like the sandcastles, the heaps and piles and mountains of chipped granite lie inert. And with no-one setting foot up there the giant clock lies about the time after years of slowly slipping backwards. The time that Aelwyn saw on its face could be days, even weeks behind.

Aelwyn checked for cars at the crossroads, emerged from paradise. The horrible dual carriageway hid the village from potential visitors years ago, secreting it in its saddlebags like contraband. The cars on the carriageway were louder than any car that might choose to come through, even at night when their engines, roaring and bubbling left to right and right to left, widened the gap between the village and that road. Aelwyn crossed and turned right, past a grey and beaten building slumped down between its neighbours with slate dripping from its brow. He stopped and looked inside, leaning closer with his hand to wipe away dust from glass that wasn't there. He toppled over and his cane dropped, landing beside him while the dust settled around. He coughed dust, sending up more clouds creating more coughs, until he pulled himself onto his backside, bad leg stretched out in front of him. The cracked paint on the walls was discoloured where crates should have been; two shades of the same colour like the apples that were there, all red but not the same. He felt wet on his head and looked around for rain or a leak in the ceiling.

– Come on, Aelwyn, brysiwch!

A woman, her hair in a bun perched high on the back of her head, dragged a small boy in. He wore brown shorts and an off-white shirt a few sizes too big was tucked into them. His knees showing below the shorts were mud stained.

14

– What have I told you about wrestling in the park? Don't!

She slapped him on the side of the head and as they passed Aelwyn saw mud on the back of his shirt.

– Now I need more soap to get these clothes clean. She checked a well-stocked shelf for whatever soap she needed, while the boy rummaged around in the crates of fruit by the window.

– Mam, can I have an apple?

– Do you have money? Good, you can buy this soap.

Aelwyn grabbed his cane and struggled hurriedly to his feet, wanting to ask the woman something, or just to look at her to see if it was her, but they walked behind him to the counter and when he turned they were gone. So was the fruit. He rubbed his head and his hand came away red. It was slowly getting dark. He stepped out through the once-window and walked to the Spar.

He shuffled up and down the aisles with a basket, on which he hooked his walking stick, and dropped in a loaf of bread, some milk, and a bag of apples. His leg was throbbing like a drum by the time he reached the medicine aisle. There was a two-for-one offer on ibuprofen and paracetamol in all of their various multicoloured offerings, each promising stronger and faster pain relief than the last. He could feel his leg wanting him to grab a few boxes of them, ignored it and dropped a box of plasters into the basket.

At the queue-less counter a bored looking girl started scanning and the turquoise numbers flashed on the screen. Milk 2.30 Bread 1.70 Apples 1.50 Plasters 3.99 and the girl said,

– Nine pounds forty nine, with a sigh.

She fingered an earring piercing a red and swollen looking lobe, scratching flakes of skin from it while Aelwyn rummaged in his pockets for change. With a handful of coins he counted nine pounds sixty and prepared to pour the coins into the girl's hands. Her hands were still by her sides.

– Don't you have a card?

– Well, yes, but I have the change here.

He held his hands out again.

– Fine.

She took the change, dropped it to the counter and began counting it, slowly. She stopped a moment and started again. Aelwyn asked for a bag and the girl slammed one down on the counter, then started counting again. He bagged up his purchases. With a grunt the girl threw the coins in the till. Aelwyn left.

Outside he checked his phone, which was still blurry in the dim light, but it hadn't tried to get his attention anyway. Walking away from the crossroads he lit another cigarette to prepare for the last climb. His stick led the way up the hill, steeper than the last but shorter. At the top he stopped and looked left to the metal structures his boys used to play on, before they had phones that they could ignore. Now the smooth and brightly coloured shapes and slides were brown and jagged, rust falling from them. Aelwyn dropped the cigarette stub to the pavement, ground it down, and dragged himself hanging from his stick up his moss slick steps. His key pierced the door and he swung in, swung it shut, dropped the key in a basket. In the kitchen the food went away, and in the bathroom he plastered his head and wiped away the red. Through to the lounge he clicked the television on, and the small faux-wooden sided box hummed and flashed until people were standing on a patch of grass, one right in the middle looking at the ground, then a flag, then the ground and back. He swung his club and people clapped reservedly. Aelwyn slumped in his brown armchair, the back above his head and the arms surrounding him. As he did every night he escaped to those green patches of grass, in his hands not a cane but a club. A ringing went off beside him and he shushed it, distracting him from the green, but it didn't stop and he picked it up. He pushed the middle button and held it to his ear.

– Dad? Came a voice.

His face softened and the flashing box was forgotten

– Hi Danny. Been waiting all day for you to call. You said you would call earlier.

– Yeah, sorry Dad. Listen, about –

– So when are you coming up to see your old dad?

– That's what I'm phoning about.

– Because I need to know how much meat I need to buy. I bet the boys are big now, so they probably eat quite a bit, don't they?

– Yeah Dad, about that –

– Have you been watching the golf? I've only just got in not ten minutes ago so I missed the first half an hour-ish.

– Dad! Let me just say something and then we can talk about whatever you want.

– Ok. What is it?

– Well, the boys have been invited to a birthday party this weekend, which is when we were planning to come up to see you, and I took my holidays this week to make time to come, but now there's this party and the boys are really looking forward to it.

– Well that's alright, you can come next week.

– That's what I was saying Dad, I took my holidays this week, and it's a relatively new placement I'm at so I'd rather not take the Mick and mess them around about moving my holidays and anyway me and Lin have made plans to go away for one night y'know because we don't really get much time to ourselves.

– But what about the boys?

– They're going to stay with Lin's parents. It's only one night.

– Oh ok. So, next week then yeah? It'll give me time to –

– No Dad, I said. I have to work next week.

– A few weeks then? Even more time. I can tidy up the spare room so the boys can have separate rooms. I suppose they do at home. What's the new house like?

– It's nice. I'll send you some pictures. Anyway I better go, Dad. Lin's just put food out.

– Ok lad. So I'll see you in a few weeks.

A pause and some quiet, faraway speech.

– Yeah, I'll phone you soon. Bye Dad.

– Bye son.

The phone beeped. He put it on the arm of the chair, picked up his cigarettes and lit one, taking a long drag down his constricting throat. The ash fell into the tray. The green grass was replaced by a large white house with huge bay windows. The words Tŷ Coch Retirement Home in faded white lettering, with a phone number under them. People were speaking but their words were useless. Aelwyn just looked at the television. The golf came back.

The red sun finally dropped below the horizon behind his head, leaving the room to take on the slight green hue of the screen. A camera flash from the observing crowd bounced from a gilded frame on the mantelpiece, drawing Aelwyn's eye. A black and white head was trapped inside that frame, whitened hair in a neat bun and slightly crowded teeth shining out into the room.

– The sun was nice tonight, Pam.

The golfers continued.

– Someone needs to do something about those chalets. They used to be so colourful.

17

He trailed off, eyes pointed at neither the golf nor the frame.

– Fell over today too, right into Mrs Davies' groceries! That hurt my leg, but we had a good laugh about it, me and Mam. And that hill from the beach nearly killed me, thought I was going to join you! He laughed and the light bouncing from the frame reflected in a stream down his cheek. He coughed. He was quiet then, watching another player take his shot. The club swung and the camera panned to follow the little dark speck as it flew hundreds of yards through countryside. He watched it fly over his head, through the grey clouds above and felt it as it thudded on the green. A perfect shot. He'd not made one as good as that before. Behind the green he saw a white house surrounded by flowerbeds, and at the tall front doors stood a woman. Her hair was tied back shone gold in the sunlight. She smiled and waved to him, the light breeze moving the hem of her dress. She walked back inside. Aelwyn took another drag on his cigarette, but stopped with half-filled lungs. He tapped it out on the ashtray and dropped it there. He exhaled, the white smoke blurring the television screen.

– I'll see you soon, Pam.

He cooked something and ate it and time passed with every swing the golfers took. The players played poorly while he chewed and swallowed and watched. The golf finished and he switched off the television, and dragged his leg upstairs.

In bed the summer heat, lingering in the dark, pushed the duvet down from his body. He shuffled left and right, tossing and turning, and then stopped. The noise from his skin on the sheets fled under the door and the silence set in. It pushed against his head, and down on top of him. The sound of blood pumping around his head beat in his ears, louder and louder, until it sounded like sand pouring in through every orifice of the room, slowly piling up around him. He felt suspended in the room, weightless.

– Be with you soon, Pamela. Don't you worry.

Then he dropped.

Jane Levy

Truth

And this is what she said had happened.

'Yes it does,' he had stated solemnly.

'Does what?' she had responded, surprised out of her own world.

'Go!' He had smiled and laughed simultaneously tossing a curl off his face. They had both been looking at a battered camper van parked on a street in a shabby but leafy suburb of an unfamiliar town in the North West.

'Tea?' he had offered as if they had been good friends for many years having one of those lazy May afternoon conversations friends care-freely have. He hadn't waited for an answer and she'd found herself following him in to a semi-detached house she had never been to in her life, feeling as if something life-changing and magnificent was about to start but for what reason, she could not say. He had apparently led her into an untidy kitchen and put on the kettle in an overly gay manner of one happy to have a surprise visit from a friend and she had complied with the scene. As he moved, she had taken a closer look at him wondering if perhaps he thought he knew her. The picture she carefully detailed was of a young male of about my age, tall and very slim with longish blond curly hair boyishly growing, undisciplined. His face she described with the finesse of a master as one which was fine featured but lacked acquaintance with its own beauty, a rare quality making her feel at ease and at once charmed.

I shuffled on my plastic chair, absurdly choosing to take on the appearance of one friend listening to another's weekend news despite my pin striped suit, English accent and gender. The pressing questions I needed answering, seemingly out of place and stark against the rich tapestry she wove, had been set aside in favour of her account. I glanced at my watch, the expensive minutes of my profession mounting up for the public purse and ventured quietly, 'And then?' although I knew many of the official answers to those two words but had not heard a trace of them from her dry lips.

She looked at me, smiling a little surprised by my youthful discomfort, brushed a greying strand from her plain face and continued the well-known lyrics in her song-like Scottish lilt, my presence being of little relevance or interest anyway. Tea ready, we made our way to an overgrown garden, which looked like a secret gardener had been carefully tending each plant to ensure it conformed to a Garden of Eden like state rather than complete disarray. As we sat drinking our warm sweet tea, he chatted on about the various plants in the garden as if he knew each on a personal basis. I said little as it didn't seem necessary to add or subtract from the stream of joy, which came from his lips. All the while, there was no question of the oddness of my being there with him and I was careful not to break the serene sense of peace, which clung like dew to every leaf.

As the sun began to set, I remained in that garden of that unfamiliar house in that area I didn't know as if I had lived there a lifetime. People, friends, faded in and out and each he greeted with new delight and they would exchange fleeting snippets of perfect chatter as I just sat there watching, not seemingly out of place but neither participating.

Evening came and we went into a lounge, which displayed a rich array of interesting things. Postcards of beautiful places were in amongst objects from distant countries and it all mixed into a cocktail of wonder. What struck me most was the innocence of the pleasure all seemed to experience and an absence of newspapers, television and radio edited the space of any violence, destruction or concern ordinary homes unconsciously convey. There were piles of unopened letters on a table in the corner but they appeared to be there, rather than anywhere else, because that was the place for letters and not because they contained any information to be neglected.

From what I could gather, when night came drawing a close to that first most wondrous day, she had followed him into his bedroom and he had read to her until she'd fallen asleep, fully clothed and utterly content. The most deeply satisfying feast of sleep had consumed her and when she'd finally woken, she had found herself nestled in the crook of his arm just in the way it should be between two people who adore each other's presence. The way she related these things remained consistently magical but monotone, only sometimes being interjected with an anarchic word

20

which was clearly her own but completely out of keeping with his poetic script.

Her fantasy took me to a place where time abided by different rules. Against the pale green and magnolia backdrop of the room in which we sat, a vision of a time emerged when past and future seemed irrelevant to the moment and no planning ever seemed to have intruded the few verbal exchanges she'd reported that they'd had. The naturalness of living in a bubble of joy had hypnotised her and the template of her being had fallen away to just being; being with him and being subjected to his ecstasy of existence. To fill in the blank time of her disappearance and to leave no detail unaccounted for, she painted a pastoral scene of picnics, swimming in blue lakes and tasting all the pleasures being human has to offer with the innocence of children conscious of nothing other than how wonderful these moments were for him and, by her memory, made equally fantastic for her. Her former life, and his, seemed of no matter to him, not from lack of caring she emphasized, but rather because of his clear euphoria of her company.

Occasionally she would glance down at her neatly folded hands, stop speaking then raise her eyes to the ceiling as if concentrating hard to retain the intricate image of him that she had formed in her mind; an image etched in beatified sand and in danger of being swept by a cruel and sudden wind. And I, yes I, despite my duty to be objective and abide by the facts dispassionate to emotion, desperately wanted to stem that wind and protect her, and the almost obscenely innocent product of their appalling union gurgling ignored in its plastic cot, from that time soon to come when Avalon would come tumbling down and the sudden sharp knowledge of the scars of her unspeakable injuries would start cracking through the surface of serenity like the ugliest of weeds forcing themselves through the sacred soil of paradise; that time when horror would replace ecstasy and spread across her face like ten thousand dominoes cascading, unstoppable.

Jane Levy

Us

We are born. We scream. Who comes first, I cannot tell.

I am three. This little girl is always near me. We probably play a lot but I don't have the words to express what we do, just images of her awkwardness and laughter in the back of my mind.

I am six. I feel her breath. We have become almost inseparable. It's not that I like her that much but I have to accept that she will be difficult to get rid off. We go to the same school and, to be honest, at times I find her a bit of an embarrassment. She isn't a dainty pretty thing, not how I'd like to see myself. She can be a bit clumsy but desperately wants to be a ballerina. With that kind of body, I doubt she ever will. Dressing up in tutus isn't enough but she doesn't seem to get it that she needs the grace and poise I have.

I am thirteen. She is always close; the only peace we get from each other is when we sleep. She is tall and has those looks that mean that she is often mistaken for a boy. I am more feminine so I get her to experiment with makeup but her eyes just go all puffy. I advise her on fashion but her stupid mum seems to always get it wrong and she still looks silly. At school she is teased all the time and I hide so that they won't see me. I suppose I abandon her.

I am sixteen. She is well developed and has a boyfriend who says he loves her whereas I am still a child, afraid of his needs. When he's not with her she longs for him, waiting for the next caress, the next kiss, the next thrill. This ache is so intense she wants to be with him all the time. I tag along. Although the whole thing is new for me too, I find myself drifting. She has become a slave to her desires while I have become her prisoner. I wait until she is away from him and strike. They are no more.

I am nineteen. We have left home and she is mine. I reckon I can do what I want but she has other ideas. She cannot go anywhere without attention and I follow to every party, every gathering and watch as she gives herself over to her senses. We enter a haze of alcohol and smoke and find ourselves in strange beds with little memory of our previous night's delight. Sometimes, though, I hate her and she clearly despises me.

I am twenty-five. I am married and so is she. How this happened I'm not quite sure. She has followed her need to be always touched, to feel safe. This isn't how we'd imagined our future. We have a baby coming and joy mixes with terror as we wonder how we will cope. Independence has been cruelly replaced by dependence. The woman no longer turns heads, the intellectual is deposed by biology and ambition clipped by expectation.

I am thirty-two. We now have two children. She is permanently exhausted and I am numbed to anything other than loving my children. The toll of childbirth on her is evident but she glows with pleasure at these two small beings that take up all her time. The tangled silken threads of our existence have been woven into a garment that is admired by all but which chafes; pleasure and pain are one. We are no longer sure where the fabric of us stops and the gown of mother begins.

I am forty. Our children are teenagers and starting to pull away. We begin to unrobe fearing what we will see. We have more time together and we aren't quite sure what we should do with it. We have forgotten what we like to do. I look at her. Her age is showing so I take her shopping and our teenage roles re-emerge. I suggest, she tries on, looks ridiculous, so we try again until we're both happy with the result. It will have to do. We laugh, hope flickers.

I am seventy. We are in a bedroom and look in to a long mirror. I examine her reflection and remember her youthful beauty which neither she nor I understood back then. I want her to travel the world, climb mountains, make love to handsome men and frolic in the most freedom we've ever had. She is tired. We look in to this mirror and she looks away, shamed by the slavery she enforces on me.

This body and I.

Jane Levy

Two Women, One Day

At 2.00 am your cold lips gently touch my cheek
I smile contented
You're here again my little one
To pull me from my sleep

At 7.00 am, her alarms go as he digs her in the ribs. She clutches sleep so at 7.05 am, he digs her again.
'Are you making coffee?' he booms.
At 7.07 am, the last thread of sleep breaks and she pulls herself up to start another day. The first drag of tobacco sends a rush to her head, the second invites the third and the fourth is not enough. The first cup of coffee shuts him up, the second warms her throat, the third signals it is time to dress and face another world. She smiles.

At 10.35 am again you come
Your cold lips brush my cheek.
Have you been let outside to play?
Come, come inside and warm yourself
Against this bitter day

At 11.00 am, people meet, people greet, people talk, people smile. She smiles. Her phone rings for the fifth time. She answers, nods and says, 'Okay, okay, I will.' A ripple of resignation crosses her face.
At 11.30 am, her small frame bends then pulls itself straight.

At 1.45 pm your cold lips are near to me
Come out so I can see!
What is it my love, my little one?
Do you want to play with me?

At 3.50 pm, the day moves on, interspersed with laughter, tea, work and chatter. People come in, go out, everyone happy, easy to please. She looks at her watch and into the evening. Resignation crosses her face. Her phone rings again. He booms resignation into her face.

At 4.10 pm my little one's cold lips touch mine
Why now, why here?
What do you want?
Go back to play divine

At 5.00 pm, she is back at home turning on her favourite lamp. The children come in and talk of their day. She hugs them hard and they say they can't breathe. She makes dinner and the dog licks his chops.

At 6.25 pm, the key is in the door and he is back. He switches a light on, the lamp is switched off. 'Is there food?' he booms and she, resigned, does as she is asked to shut him up.

At 7.35 pm your cold lips tease me
I look around to see
But you stay hidden in the shadows
Just tinkling with glee

At 8.00 pm, the evening TV starts and she goes to smoke. The first drag offers silence, the second peace, the third takes the first two promises away and the fourth begs for them back. 'Is there any wine?' he booms and she trots to the shop to shut him up.

The first glass sends a rush to her head, the second already invites the third and the fourth is just not enough. Eventually, a place of possibilities finds her and she smiles again.

'Is there more?' he booms.

The smile switches off, resignation sweeps across her face and she gives him another to shut him up.

At 11.07 pm your dead lips kiss my cheek
Why are you up so late my sweet?
You should be snuggled in your bed
With teddy resting by your lovely head
Let's go to sleep together
So that we can always be near
Let's dream of lovely places
Where there are no more tears

At 11.32 pm, she is drunk and he's still by the telly. She quietly slips up to the bed to lie on her belly.

L. Windridge

Dirty Words

In the Beginning

Everything begins with words.

On the pale sand a low, goat hair tent is held up by sticks. The cloth billows like wind across the desert and ragged flags beckon outside. The storyteller mends one of his puppets. They remind Maria of her neighbours.

A young man watches her hips swing under her loose garment as she carries her jug on her head to the well.

There is sweat on the cloth covering the cave of her underarm. He wants to tuck away the strands of dark hair which stick wetly across her cheek, kiss her, touch her skin and see her smile – again.

But he knows she is afraid.

Water spills as she sets down the jug.

'Meet me,' he hisses, 'At the salt caves.'

It is forbidden but she likes how he makes her feel powerful.

The storyteller stops sewing for a moment.

The power of the highest shall overshadow thee.

Maria walks out of sight and hides her anklet of bells.

She slinks close to the village wall and springs up loose steps. From up here her neighbours look smaller and for a moment she feels omnipotent. She can hear the flags flapping in the distance. A snake shifts in the thin dry grass. She imagines the conversation in the street.

'There is foul breath putrefying my goat's milk.'

'Why does your daughter scream? The old woman died last night they say. Was it evil eye, Imma?'

Her mother's head is cowed in shame at the accusing finger.

Sickened Maria kicks a pebble that scuds down the steps before she turns to run down the slope. Stones smash into pieces on the hillside where a goat stands impossibly balanced to lick the rock face. Maria squeezes into a cold, dark hole and feeling the wall with the flat of her hands she creeps along passageways of saline rock.

Crystalline pinpoints rise above her, sparkling in the shafts of sunshine that penetrate the strange white darkness. She stops, entombed in the cold air and awful magnificence. Perhaps she should go back. They will be asking where she is. Then bending low she looks behind a pillar and he is right there. She laughs with delight and then muffles the sound with her shawl.

Her feet are silent on the white sand; rays of light are directly above her. He takes her hand and pulls her to him. Relief embraces and caresses away her fear.

'A goddess,' he whispers as she gives herself up. Their bodies so close that not a word or a breath would fit between them. Her eyes water as she stares at the sunrays behind his shoulder. He licks her face, stiffens and exhales – it is done.

She squeezes out from under him and vomits. She is thirteen years old.

'Don't tell,' Maria says.

'Meet me again.'

'Lech, leave me alone.'

He holds his hands up, obediently,

'Say nothing, then no one can ever know,' he says leaving, hand over his mouth. Crouching on her haunches, she miauls quietly.

Her mouth tastes vile.

No words, no story. No words, no death.

She will not speak.

Fear Not Mary.

Words make a story, truth is a different matter.

Words buy dates at the market, it's how children learn, it's how stories are spread and history is told. People talk, women die.

Eating a crust of bread to calm the morning sickness and blood iron taste, I run to the stands. There's dust and cloth and shouting.

Last year, on my twelfth birthday, Ruben tortured a pregnant cat. He held her down and cut off her ears and her tail. I remember the bloody stump. She screeched so much he cut her throat.

Jostling close to me is a man smelling of sweat and piss and I hear chanting and wailing far off.

Then I see the woman, her eyes are like the cat's. Held on either side, she strains. I want to look at the woman, who is like me, but not like me. But I want to look away too.

27

She miauls and spits at the man who smells of piss.

'I knew you'd do this, the moment you touched me,'

He wipes his face. She looks at me for a moment, as if she can see inside me, then I see her dark eyes roll white, as if giving up on both our lives.

She cowers. Dogs sniff one another at the wall.

The stones hit her flesh. First a graze and then deeper. I had imagined it would be different. That blood would flow and inside her would be pure white bones but it was fat meat that was crushed and seeping from beneath the dark skin.

'Zonna, Slut.'

I watch as her legs crumple, knocked out sideways, awkward. Her body falls as shards skim the ground. Her fingers loosen and under her nose is a gouge of blood snot.

A smell rises from her bowels.

It is finished.

I curl my arms round my secret and feel the fear in my stomach. I would tell any story, but I won't let that happen to me.

There is dust and cloth and blood and madness. A boy throws a stone to break up the rutting dogs. They yelp and skulk away up an alley.

I was hit by a sharp stone once.

'Ruben did it,' I screamed. Imma was furious and beat him.

'Don't throw stones,' she said.

Iron has entered my soul and I can taste it.

Then Joseph, being a just man, and not willing to make her a public example, was minded to put her away privily.

A cock crows, out of place, at night. Imma strokes Maria's hair to calm her yelling.

'Quiet!' shouts a neighbour through the wall.

A goat brays.

'No moon-time yet?' Imma thinks. She has noticed how her daughter eats only dry crusts.

She hums just for the two of them, an ancient song about a girl, Leda.

Earlier that evening, Maria had crouched with Ruth on threadbare rugs and listened to the storyteller. From the baskets of dates sticky stones are spat on the sand, they will be little dried

28

pellets tomorrow, flesh all gone. Close by another girl scratches her skin through cloth. Ruth pulls Maria to sit further away. Goat fat spits on the fire. Tonight the story is about a young girl and an incubus.

'Every night, he devours her.' The storyteller raises the puppets' arms.

'Heavy dark wings crushing the air, his weight like a stone cracking, foul breath drowns her. Her flesh taut in pain and shamelessness, noise sucked away.'

Some women look behind them, but they feel safe here. Maria barely breathes, her mouth still tastes vile.

'The girl's an animal.' The storyteller is leaning forward taking the audience into his confidence. Maria waits for him to point at her.

'Remember the old mother, tended by her family at night. With her last rattling breaths, her lips murmur and she reaches out to touch something.'

He sees their faces pale, and their eyes suspiciously avoid one another's. He sits back and scratches the lice in his hair and wraps himself in his blanket. He recognises some of them from the well where he'd drawn water, his head covered like a woman, eavesdropping on the gossip before he returned to tell his stories.

Ruth won't walk to the well with Maria next morning, instead she'll whisper with her friends.

Imma remembers how Anna thumped her abdomen with hatred. She took poisonous herbs. She screamed like a cat as she miscarried.

Her father left and went to the hills.

Maria should go to the hills.

The sun was up when Imma was turning flatbreads and the cockerel was killed and hung from the tree.

From her doorway she saw the puppeteer and a young man leave. They slapped one another's backs laughing, talking, telling stories.

When Herod the king had heard these things he was troubled and all Jerusalem with him.

Two years later, I press my finger to my lips. My boy copies, I nod.

Soldiers shout outside and we are squeezed in the gap. The flat grey sheets of rock bear down above us. A strip of cold white sand reminds me of home.

Quiet. Don't speak.

29

'Sssshssssh,' he enjoys the sound. I shake my head, my eyes wild. I pick him up and clasp his face tight to my body,

Quiet. He gasps for air, I put him down and bending low to his height, hold my hand up and again put my finger to my lips. I cover his hair with my shawl and roll it over his mouth, his eyes glisten.

Outside in the loud sunlight they are searching. They have split the tent poles, torn the cloth. I can smell their sweat and hear the goats running back and forth.

'Show me you're a girl.'

Laughter, someone hawks spit. The women's voices are unheard as their boys are ripped from them.

My lucky son now has a hundred mothers.

Sssshsssh.

His eyes search mine.

Why Immaleh?

I close my eyes.

How would I explain the child held upside down? Terror in his eyes, disbelieving hands held out, convulsive crying choked. His throat cut, his suddenly limp, plump body tossed onto a cart.

My boy bows his head next to me in this damp gap of life. We speak without speaking.

Why Immaleh?

I don't know. Be still!

I can't. He wriggles free of my grip.

You have to.

My knees hurt. I have slipped down onto my haunches, hard rock against my spine and knees and forehead. I am bent with fear. I am bent with protecting him. My body and my mantle always surround him.

Comfort me.

And what if I can't? What if I pull away and run, what if I just hand him over? Gently from my arms to theirs.

Don't do it.

His small limbs nudge at me. His eyes flickering under dark lids speak to me.

Do it for me, his milky joined-to-me smell rips me open because he is me, and he is not me.

Protect me above yourself, for yourself, because I am you. And that's what we do. That's what we do.

But Rachel laid her son down screaming and ran.

Immaleh?

She ran away and killed herself and I understand.

He opens his eyes and sees the uncertainty in mine, he sees my fear. His body stiffens with rage. For me, for him, I change my look within, because any gap or crack in that and he will see right into it.

Behold the handmaid of the Lord.

Look at Maria's child now as he runs towards her his unblemished feet on the sand. He is rare among us tortured women. In the cool of the tent we share our meal with him, olives, bread, melon, honey. The breeze flaps the pale cloth. I pick out the lemon in the cracked water jug and suck its bitterness to cleanse my mouth and then the others come singing up the hillside. I spit out a pip.

Maria stoops and he seeks out and fingers her dark hair under the white veil and hopes that she smiles. He washes in the copper bowl where a big yellow sun shines,

'Imma,' he coughs, eyes closed, hands held out. She wipes his face with the cloth of her dress. Cupping her hands, she scoops water for herself.

A young woman is rubbing her bleeding sores through her white gown.

'Lechi,' her mother slaps her hand. She knows we sometimes push people out.

And then they are ready for him.

Maria is going to pass his soul, his mind and his body into the priest's arms. She doesn't hesitate as she climbs the steps hewn into the rock where the priest is standing.

'Ssssh, ssssh.'

Just the rustle of the tree, our garments and the smell of incense in the heat.

And all that heard him were astonished at his understanding and answers.

He starts to cry.

A cloud moves across the sky. The high leaning cliffs rise up and the boy is taken away.

His scream is blood curdling, echoing like the call of the kestrel before a kill. His legs kick the priest with rage, arms held out to his mother. But Maria is walking away; someone is waiting to wash her

31

feet. Later they will start initiating the boy in secret. Secrecy protects us.

'It is God's will.

To cleanse the earth.'

What would make a woman do that? It makes me hiss and grit my teeth but I am as afraid of the priests as if they were blood-crazy soldiers and my voice is lost in the chanting,

'Bless the women who give up their sons.

Bless all the chaste women,

Willing to give their sons.'

Later in the darkness, I slip down the scree to the well. The woman is still there rubbing her sores. I lower my bucket into the black water where the reflection of the moon is surrounded with moss and fungus. The storyteller asks me what happened and I tell him.

Emma Hutson

Remember?

The house smells different as I walk in the front door. It smells like unrequited lust and homework due in tomorrow. There are shoes in the hallway, platforms really, well worn, all frayed laces and ripped tongues. A coat hugs the banister, leather, long, scuffed along the bottom where the hem has dropped.

She's on the sofa, slouched into the corner of the seat, legs out, crossed at the ankle, one arm across her stomach, the other reaching up to play with the ball at her lip. She looks up through a too-long-fringe, kohl-rimmed eyes peering past too-dark-hair. I'd forgotten the black lipstick, erased it from memory and photo-albums alike. She raises an eyebrow and quirks her mouth in an almost smile; she's wondering what she's supposed to say. 'Tea?' I ask. She nods and stands; it's polite to offer tea when you have a guest, it was drilled into us when we were younger, when I was a lot younger.

The kettle rattles in the corner of the kitchen; she stands there on the linoleum in odd socks and baggy jeans, flares. She tugs at the bottom of the billowing shirt, God. I'd forgotten that shirt, tried to anyway. I wore it for Halloween this year. The mugs are on the side, one sugar in mine, an avalanche in hers; no wonder I never used to sleep.

It's hard to remember how she must be feeling right now, this is the time when they pulled the shell off of the snail and expected it to live as a slug. The kettle rattles against its base and I lift it up before it clicks. Impatience, that's something that's never changed. Stirring the tea I fumble for something to say. God this is awkward.

She accepts the mug, I pass it to her handle first, but she still holds the mug itself, our fingers touch. They use that in romance novels as some sort of flirty gesture, it's actually just awkward; fingers slipping over fingers, the cup tilting, almost sloshing tea over the side. We giggle, the same intoned exhaling of breath, the same wincing smile. This is ridiculous. 'Don't worry' I want to say, 'it all works out in the end, admittedly not the way you're imagining now. There's no forensics in your future, no Him either. It wasn't the science you loved; it was the novels about it. You're going to write, or try to, you're going to disappoint yourself and wonder why words abandon you, why they make you chase them, when they know you can't run. But don't worry, I'm ok, see? All grown up, you made it, we made it.' But I don't. She'd only roll her eyes and think that I'm lying, or an idiot. There's always the prospect of messing up the fabric of time too, laddering the nylons of the universe, and I'm fresh out of clear nail varnish.

'How's school?' A shrug. 'Still have that crush on your maths teacher?' God, what's her name? She frowns, sips at the steaming tea. I should warn her about the fillings she's going to have to get. She rubs her lips together thinking of something to say. 'This is a nice house.' Phone voice, posher than regular conversation.

'Thanks. Not how you'd decorate it I'm sure.'

'Maybe some more colour, but this is nice. My mum always does cream with coloured accents.' I should ask her something else, something less mumsy and pathetic.

'Come with me, you'll love this.' I take her upstairs, we both spill our tea on the carpet, always have, it's why I chose brown for the hallway. I open a door and flip on the light, standing to the side so that she can get the full effect.

'You have a library?' She looks around, trying to hold in a smile that would expose the braces.

'It's even full of books you'd actually want to read, not just the posh boring ones that we pretend to be interested in.' She snorts and walks to a shelf, tilting her head to read the spines.

'Dickens?'

'He's actually not as bad as you'd think, honestly. I was surprised too.'

A scornful 'Hmm,' I always did argue with myself.

*

I've never been a fan of science fiction; I mean, I've watched Star Wars, but who hasn't? So you can imagine what a mystery it was when I walked in to find her there. I did think that maybe I was asleep, or that I'd taken too many paracetamol during the day. A brain tumour never occurred to me.

*

'Why do all of these guys have such small dicks?'

34

'It was the fashion at the time for sculptures.'

'What, to like, save money on marble? Is that why Venus doesn't have arms? Because that's just cheap.'

'*Suzanne!* And for goodness sake, could you at least *pretend* that you're not eating popcorn in the gallery?'

'I would *definitely* ask for his number.'

'He's from ancient Greece; he wouldn't have had a phone, or even have known what one was.'

'Will you stop ruining my fantasy with all of your stupid logic please.' A shared grin, some stolen popcorn, the resting of a hand on a shoulder.

'Fine, once you had his number what would you do?'

'Um, obviously call him, ask him out on a date, to see...gladiators or, I don't know, storm Troy or something.' An explosive laugh, a hand to the mouth as if she could draw the noise back in.

'Aside from the way in which you just completely raped historical fact, they don't sound like very romantic options for a first date.'

'No, but they do sound exciting don't they? And if there's one thing a dying girl wants it's a little excitement in her life.' A dropped smile, dragging the rest of the body down with it onto a nearby bench. 'Oh and cake, lots of cake. Come on Maria, let's roll! Well, I'll roll, you push, but onwards! Towards cake!' An arm outstretched, sternly pointing forwards, the face of an emperor leading his men to war, a hand delving into a bag of popcorn.

*

The sun forces its way through autumn clouds and London smog to fall in bleary patches on uneven pavements. Damp leaves cling to their wheels and shoes, and grimy water flicks itself up Maria's jeans.

'Your chair is ruining my Levis.'

'You got them on eBay anyway.'

*

So, I've asked them to read this out during the funeral; I did entertain thoughts of doing a video and literally talking to you from beyond the grave, but I thought that might be a little too much. I just wanted to let you know that it's ok, and that I don't have any regrets, except for the whole hair-dye debacle of '92, sorry about ruining the wedding photos Eloise.

I had a while to prepare for this, so I've gone over the plans thoroughly, and none of you are to argue. I've got a white coffin for a reason; there should be some permanent markers at the altar. Get doodling! Just think of it as a giant plaster-cast.

There's a party after the service, sort of like a wake, but with shots instead of cucumber sandwiches. Nan, I'll let you off with a sherry, but the rest of you, you're obligated to do a shot of tequila I'm afraid, salt and all.

Well, I won't drag this out too long, I'm sure you're all dying to sing 'all things bright and beautiful', (get it? Dying! Too much? Oh well.)

Love and kisses.

*

'I'm thinking about getting a tattoo.'

'Of what?'

'Don't know, doesn't matter really, I'm not going to have time to regret it.' A cup drops into a saucer with a clink.

'Must you always make it into a joke? This is serious Suzanne. It's not funny, not everything can be funny.' A shuddering sigh.

'I could get piercings too.'

'Why aren't you angry?'

'Maybe one of those bull ones? Through the middle bit of my nose.'

'*I'm* angry. I'm so fucking angry, Suzanne! Why aren't you? Why aren't you out there hating old people, just because *they* get to *be* old? I don't understand how you can be so calm, I don't understand, Suze.' A deep breath, a slow exhalation. 'It's not fair, and I don't understand it.' Silence falls over the table as the women stare into their cups and blink hard, a pale hand with purple nails reaches to cover the one with the French manicure. The cafe bustles around them.

'Did you know that you can get pink gravestones?'

'You don't like pink.'

'I don't like mice either but I'm still going to be buried with a load of them.'

'What? Why?'

'If Time Team digs me up in 200 years I want them to think that I was the pied piper.' A perfectly serious face opposite the spluttering of tea into a napkin.

'So, what tattoo are you going to get?' Peace offering, olive branch, no dove, but plenty of pigeons outside.

'I don't know. Angel wings on my arse?'

*

Dear Annabelle,

I've written so many drafts of this letter, but they all ended up so dreary and morbid, and I don't want you to get the wrong impression of me, I'm not a fogey, I promise. I've decided that the best thing to do is to just share my favourite memory of you, it only happened a couple of months ago; you're six months old as I write this. Anyway, we were in town doing some shopping in the sales; your mum had you strapped to her chest in one of those weird harness things. We were in this huge queue, completely loaded down with baskets of clothes, and all of a sudden you let loose this rip-roaring fart. The entire shop went silent. It was a proper grown up fart, honestly, it sounded like it came from a 70 year old, lactose intolerant man (smelt like it too), so of course no one believed that it was you, they all thought it was your mum. She went so red. We actually had to leave the shop, baskets and all. I could tell from that fart that you're going to grow up just fine, a strong figure of a woman if ever I saw one.

I've been told that it's tradition to impart advice to one's goddaughter, I started to try and write something, but it ended up being more confusing than reading Byron with a hangover. I decided bullet points would be easier for all involved:

- Don't read Shakespeare, watch it, even if it's just at the local theatre or on DVD. Shakespeare never intended for his works to be read, and as we all know, you never argue with a man in pantaloons.
- Lists will save you every time. Never trust your memory. You may think that you'll remember something, but inevitably you won't. Lists, lots of them. Also, on that note, you should keep a diary. Life is insane; beautifully,

wonderfully, sublimely insane, try to remember as much of it as you can.

- Never let a boy (or girl) push you around, you are too beautiful and too special. They say people can change, but it takes time, if they've hurt you once, it's pretty likely they'll do it again.
- Tattoos really are for life. It may seem like a great idea at the time, but make sure that it's something you'll still want when you're forty. Ask to see your Uncle Michael's arm if you're still unsure about this point, (ask anyway, it's hilarious).
- Clear nail-varnish stops ladders in tights from running further. Toothpaste gets biro stains off leather. No-more-nails really can stick a chair to the ceiling, but you won't be able to sit in it, no matter how hard you try. Oh, and, never home-bleach your hair.

Happy 18th birthday darling; look after your mum for me, even if she's doing your head in, that's a mum's job, and she's lovely really.

All of my love,
Suzanne, your godmother.

*

If you based your research on telly or films you'd imagine that getting over cancer is pretty easy. You're sick for a while, do those pale, tear-stained goodbyes, and then miraculously recover. That doesn't happen in real life. In real life you assume that those headaches are just stress, that the blurry eyes mean that you've stared at the computer too long, and that the odd wobble when you walk means that you pushed yourself too hard on the treadmill. In real life, when you go to the doctor it takes weeks for results to come back. In real life you've left it too long. In real life, you die.

*

This is the last will and testament of Suzanne Marigold Peterson.

Being of sound body and mind (or as sound as it ever got) I hereby bequeath all of my worldly junk to you poor suckers. (I did look into getting a proper will drafted, but it looked like a long and boring process, and I don't really own anything of massive value anyway, so I'm trusting you guys to manage this amongst yourselves).

Most of my stuff can go to Oxfam if none of you guys want it, but there's a few key items that I'd like to pass on.

To Annabelle, you get my silver and opal ring, I got it for my eighteenth, and I always assumed that one day it would be an heirloom. I have chunky fingers, so you might need to wear it on a necklace until you're older.

To Maria, my Jimmy Choos, I've seen you eye-balling them for years, may they cripple you just as they did me, enjoy the bunions in remembrance of me. Also, the necklace you gave me for my twenty-first, I loved it, and I told them to make sure that I wasn't wearing it when I was cremated, it wouldn't do to waste something so shiny.

Mum, you get anything you want, obviously, but you also get the ring back, you know the one. And my computer, you need a new one Mum, I know you hate the 'blasted contraptions' but you really can't get along in life without one nowadays.

*

'Tea?' She nods and leans against the kitchen counter as I fill the kettle, click it on and reach for some mugs.

'Why do you put them on the top shelf?' I smile and exhale a small laugh.

'It means that I have to stretch' at her perplexed look I continue, 'I sit at a desk all day, so I make sure that I take every opportunity to stretch my back out; I didn't want to end up one of those hunch-backed old people.' She raises her eyebrows and flashes a smile.

'Fair enough.' I hand her the now prepared tea, I hold the handle this time. Holding it up to her bottom lip she blows into the mug as though it were a flute, even though we learnt clarinet when we were at primary school. She repeats the action and I know that she's looking at the ripples that her breath creates in the amber liquid.

'I know you're not real.' She frowns looking up from her tea. 'You're here because of the tumour, in my brain. You're not actually real.'

'I feel real.'

39

'Well, yeah, because you only exist in my mind, and I'm imagining you as imagining yourself to be real.' She raises her eyebrows, the ring in the right one catches the light.

'If I'm not real, why are you talking to me?'

'Well, because you're here, we're both here stuck with one another.'

'Well, if what you say is true, then, I'm not really here, so we're not stuck. Just imagine me away.'

'Well if I were just imagining you in the first place, I would, but *I'm* not, it's the tumour.'

'So ignore me until I go away. Go have some chemo or something.'

'That'd be rude. And I can't, it's too advanced.'

'It would be rude to ignore an imaginary person, who's only there as a result of a terminal brain tumour?' I wince and nod. 'God, I really do turn into our mother.'

We grin and sip at our tea.

*

'Don't you think it's a bit morbid to tag her in photos of her own coffin and gravestone?'

'It's what she wanted. You know what she's like. Was like.'

*

Suz Peterson: As Queen said 'Who wants to live forever anyway?'
Thirty-four people like this

Comments:
Michael Gillingham: We miss you Suz. Hope you show those angels how to have a good time!
Four people like this

Georgina *G-boss* Adler: Hope that you're up there dirty dancing with Patrick Swayze!
Eight people like this

Maria Walters: It's not the same here without you, none of the Greek statues are getting propositioned. I think they miss you. You

40

would have loved your wake; even your Nan did a shot of tequila! Your coffin looks awesome. I tagged you like you asked, you dark individual.

Twenty people like this

Maria Walters: Oh, and I have blisters from those bloody shoes.

Amanda Peterson: I'd just like to thank everyone for their kind words, Suzie would have really appreciated it.

Twenty-eight people like this

*

'I know you're not real.'

'Then you probably shouldn't talk to me, Mum looks worried.'

'Mum always looks worried, that's her default look.' A smile, a hand stroking down a limp arm. 'Not long now. Tell Mum I love her.'

'I think you just did.' A glance to the woman leaning forward in the orange plastic hospital chair, tightly holding a pale hand with electric blue nails. A tear winding its way through foundation and face powder.

'Everything is going to be okay.'

Liam Johnson

Decembuary 54th

[AT 10:30AM HIS CLOCK RADIO RAISES THE ALARM]
[GROUND CONTROL TO MAJOR TOM…]

woke up from nightmares of Evie

(who received me with a chandelier of
          mascara on her eyelids and silently led me
          to an estuary of lead, where   '
          blackberries steadily bled. but   '
                              we   '   ,
          fed   "

                                                               '

on havisham fruit,
mothball suited .   '
over peals of silence   always silence in my dreams
my feelings on the
scene got convoluted & the darker of them went
                    unrefuted

                    as in moted light
                    i saw her face was bare   with
                    two black eyes   shut tight   )

and straightaway there was a pallor of clouds smurched across my brain.

mercifully the fact of the day was warm when i opened the curtains; a sun was hung from the sky and i thought about Apollo as a god of the sun, and Apollo as the name of the spacecraft.

Apollo with his fire and his lyre, the anatomy of a man without fear to rattle his alloy hand. And they liked the idea of bringing such a grand dapper dan man to lovely Selene the girl next door who sits

serene and draws sharks to the shore. sometimes i don't think she
gets the respect she deserves any more.
i wondered if they realised the cataclysms of their symbology
imagined the sun consuming the moon in fire totally sunlike
a sea full of surfers absentminded with nowhere to be dragged
an avian skull crushed at the bottom of a bag, a victim finch
of the compensatory instinct to spill blood
which would arise in the minds of the bachelor earth
as it lay under a frieze of sky full of fires and fatherhoods
with no pale girl in orbit like a comforting dream evermore

because Everest wasn't just 'there' any more, and   Mallory
suffered maladies of the cerebellum or   s o u l
which buffeted his body and ate his brain   whole

       an imbalance of torrential humours
       destruction in pursuit of a goal.

[HE SHOWS HIS FACE, DISTORTED, COLD, LIKE HIS
MIRROR IS A SPOON IN A CEREAL BOWL]

E p i F a l c o
Either lunar or more likely a loon – something to do with the
moon. Foul play.
23 Jan, 11:04 am   Delete Comment   Thumbs up

A n g e l a N e t t l e s
I watched Armageddon last night.
23 Jan, 11:23 am   Delete Comment   Thumbs up (1)

E v i e W a c h o w s k i
You can't blame the moon for the state of the loon. I'm sorry.
also nettles, I'm leaving on a jet plane.
23 Jan, 12:04 pm   Delete Comment   Thumbs up

E p i F a l c o
when the fuck will you be back again?
23 Jan, 12:15 pm   Delete Comment   Thumbs up

[AT TENPASTWELVE HE LEAVES HIS HOME]
[WHEN IN ROAM]
[DO AS THE ROAMING DO / OR BE TRULY ALONE]

       shaking the satellites out of my hair to spare myself the trouble of thoughts on the masculine and feminine at a time like this, i check the time and realise i probably have a bus to miss. piss-poor anyway. i dress, bit by bit hiding the skin and the sites of past kisses, brandishing a torch at the vision which crept and caught me carefully as i slept through the stetson night.

finishing my morning smoke, i refuse to provoke
such a chain reaction   as these reflections   might serve to evoke
     as i step outside i hear klaxon calls
     but there is no fuzz car in sight
     so i walk sunkissed down Helenstreet
     past boys on stolen bikes.

Overheard mumblists on the way say:
         'I KNOW A COUPLE OF DYKES'
     'WHEN I'M HUNGOVER I EAT RUNNY EGGS'
'ARE YOU SURE THAT'S WORD FOR WORD WHAT
                   SHE   ID' SA
     'THE POWER'S GENERATED BY
    THE FORCE OF THE TIDE'
      'BIDE YOUR TIME FUCK WITH HER HEAD'

[AT THIS POINT EPI FORGETS HIS DREAM AND]

               i glide on with autonomous legs.

   E v i e W a c h o w s k i
can't help but wake up with a sense of liberation.
23rd Jan, 9:15 am   Delete Comment   Thumbs up (1)

   A n g e l a N e t t l e s
   enjoy it :) if you start to feel like a witch, look at your lovely fingers and notice that they aren't the least bit witchlike.
23rd Jan, 9:45 am   Delete Comment   Thumbs up

Matthew Everett
They still choked the life out of that relationship though.
23rd Jan, 9:48 am   Delete Comment   Thumbs up

Angela Nettles
Matthew you're a sadistic piece of shit
23rd Jan, 9:52 am   Delete Comment   Thumbs up

Angela Nettles
pay no mind, Evie Wonder, you've done nothing wrong
23rd Jan, 9:52 am   Delete Comment   Thumbs up

Matthew Everett
DING DONG. Telegram: you cast a spell on the man with
your singsong voice. I'm not saying you made the wrong choice. But
the cruelty is undeniable. You might as well have handed him a copy
of Joyce...
23rd Jan, 9:56 am   Delete Comment   Thumbs up

[12:42] [HAVING BANISHED CLINGING THOUGHTS OUR HERO'S STOMACH SAYS RUMBLE]

i don't care how the cookie crumbled any more, there are no
bumblebees in the air but it's not on days like this that bookies take
bets on the uppersums of casualties at war. my faith restored by the
sunshine. maybe it's related to vitamin D. invisible vitamins seeping
down out of the sky and saturating me.

i head for a supermarket brunch thinking, fuck punch and
judy. all the stoners with mid afternoon munchies giggle blinking in
the aisles with their new loans and when they're obstructing me i say
'scuse' with a 'buddy' on the side, and i smile to create a good vibe. a
pair of luvbirds by the magazine racks. doesn't bother me.
his arm and her waist, a slap to my face, no harm done. i take it in
good grace. good fun.

when i take the scotch egg off the shelf a piece of paper
falls out from behind it. it's been folded up small. unable to leave it
as i found it – unfold it. hold it.

it's a poem of all things. a weirdo has been hiding weirdo
treasure in the shelves – the   universe rings my doorbell, so i turn
the handle. what the hell.   it goes
45

FINK TEST

1. 'finks are like witches but harder to see
a fink won't even float when thrown in the Dead Sea.'

2. ask to hold hands
when you're drinking
with your fink

see if it says 'no
give me a cigarette!'

its eyes like opals
cold and golf
gulfwar
whisky &
dye
and when it does –
'cause it will –
and strokes the weasel in its purse
its beard gelled slick but full of mites

knock a drink into its lap
as if by accident
& watch its face go hiss
offer it money for another &
let it bite your wrist

dagger

o your fink
with its pink nose
like a biscuit

o has it bitten you now
like a stapler

o has your fink finked out
& done what finks do best

what a way to find out
you should have done a

46

FINK TEST.

3. 'Finks are like astronauts but more in your face
because you'll still hear a fink screaming out in deep space.'

[IT IS 12:48 AND HE WALKS OUT WITHOUT PAYING]
[NOT A DELIBERATE CRIME]
[A FRAGILE PEACE SHATTERED]

[CHEST TIGHT / SCARF CONSTRICTING]
[HIS MIND BACK ON DARK MATTERS]

the populace of the park scatters when i step in which does not help
my paranoia . . .
perhaps it is down to pure chance but like dandelion seed they
disperse a hundred fathers with eyes like the Saturn of Goya
the eyes of the mothers of their sons
the corneas of lovers on the run
both beautiful and horrible to me
like one hand with a cornetto
    and one with a gun

M a t t h e w E v e r e t t
There's no knowing where Epi's going unless you know him like
I do.
23rd Jan, 2:00pm   Delete Comment   Thumbs up

D e r m o t t C o a t e s
like only a gay lover can?
23rd Jan, 2:09pm   Delete Comment   Thumbs up

A n g e l a N e t t l e s
like a shit-stirring friend?
23rd Jan, 2:12pm   Delete Comment   Thumbs up

M a t t h e w E v e r e t t
If I didn't stir the shit nobody would even notice it. Until it hits
the fan.
23rd Jan, 2:21pm   Delete Comment   Thumbs up

47

E v i e W a c h o w s k i
what are you talking about? try without smoke and mirrors?
23rd Jan, 2:24pm   Delete Comment   Thumbs up

M a t t h e w E v e r e t t
Mirrors and smoke are essentially his two favourite things, so I
don't see why we should ignore them. He'll be looking much harder
at the mirror now, in any case. That's what I'm saying. Narcissism
and pessimism are a horrible cocktail.
23rd Jan, 2:30pm   Delete Comment   Thumbs up

E v i e W a c h o w s k i
he's not answering his phone
23rd Jan, 2:45pm   Delete Comment   Thumbs up

[ONE DOT ONE ONE PM]
[THREE LINES LIKE A CRICKETWICKET]
[WITH THE BAILS KNOCKED OFF]
[ON THE FACE OF HIS DIGITAL WRISTWATCH]

when i get to the forest at the end of the park i sit down
the poem still seething at me in my skull
and wonder if i was actually believing that bullshit
before i pulled at the handle and the pit of
my stomach fell out leaving only the
pendulum of my elastic heart.
it was going to end this way from the start.
la belle dame sans circus trapeze
i played my part & caught her
like a LAMB TO SLAUGHTER
pied porter, and carried her home.
now i stare at Helios
from the dome of my observatory.
its flames are the flames of a Hindenburg
from before the first race memory.
it has outlasted its tenancy, outstayed its welcome
& WORN THIN MY ACCEPTANCE OF ITS BLAZES
WHICH MELTED THE WINGS OF ICARUS.
speaking for men in dazes, i am sorely sick of us
and we are just as sick of you.

because we are fickle
brittle and crazy
baby blue.

[HE MUMBLES THIS AS IF IT IS TRUE]
[AT ONE : ONE TWO THE UNIVERSE THINKS]
[I HAVE HAD ENOUGH OF YOU]

E v i e   W a c h o w s k i
Epi, it's over. We're through.
22nd Jan, 11:23 pm   Delete Comment   Thumbs up

upping my chin to squint blind and angry
                        at my boy soul up in its totemic Star
and beg it to reveal its plan to me i do not get that far . i have been
            the ruiner of too much without knowing why
            so Kali sends a bird like a cherub in vengeance
            with instruction to tell me i'm going to die
            and pluck out my eyes and their tendons.

[YOU SHOULD SEE HIM AT THIRTEEN PAST]   [CURLED
UP ON THE LEAFMOLD]   [CAN'T KEEP HOLD]
[OF HIS FACE HIS HANDS KEEP QUESTING FOR HELP]
[LOOSENING HIS BELT AND HOLDING HIS BALLS]
[THE NATURAL RESPONSE OF A MALE WHO FALLS]
[FROM GRACE QUITE HOPLESSLY]   [NEVER]
[FOCUSING TOTALLY ON THE ANSWER] [THOUGH HE
GLIMPSED IT UNKNOWING] [IN ITS GRANDEUR]

Ashleigh Davies

The Glass Passenger

The heat of the sun is inconsequential, what twelve year old truly cares about the weather? Twelve year old boys do no initiate conversations with the same tired lines as their elders. Whatever the weather, it is always perfect outdoors, with the crisp sweet scent of autumn just about filling my nostrils. I am a skinny child, skinny and small. My brother is much the same, almost built to scale. We have been playing in the garden, and our palms are dirty with dry muck. With no thought for suspense he unfurls his fingertips to expose another muddied palm, and sat atop it a pristine artefact. It is a toy car, a tiny thing, shiny and red with black plastic wheels.

'I found it,' he says. I smile, gently picking it up and surveying it, the doors still opened as I remembered; a little stiff maybe. The interior was caked with dried earth. We had buried that car a summer ago. I'm unsure as to the circumstances, age blurs the images, softens the angles.

I have vague recollections of that summer, of the days spent outside of the house, of playing in the garden and of imagination. The days where my brother and I would transform ourselves into gladiators, jousting at each other with branches, crouching behind the fort of the chicken coop. Did we ever keep chickens? Maybe back when Mum was around.

*

The house has grown so old now, years of grime and soot have accumulated around the stone fireplace. We never light it anymore. When we were children, Dad used to sit in the wooden rocking chair by the hearth, in the brief moments when he wasn't looking after Mum. He would go there with his pipe and find some sort of solace. I am not sure what it was that he felt when he puffed away at that pipe and stared into the softly lapping flames. I think, deep down, it may have felt something like guilt. He never spoke of his duties with Mum, at the start it was the little things, obviously. He used to help her out to the kitchen, to the stove and the kettle where she insisted she made her own tea. He couldn't make it right, according to her. Too hot, too sugary, too dark, wrong cup, wrong spoon. The kettle would whistle for minutes sometimes, but still she insisted upon the struggle from the settee to the kitchen. More often than not the tea would remain half drunk, I think it was her way of holding on to independence. Little battles. I remember when she became bedbound, the conversations we used to have.

'It's the smallest things,' she would say. 'Putting my shoes on, walking in the garden, not being able to tend to my flowers. How are my flowers?' I didn't bother going to the window to check.

'They're fine, me and Sandy got them covered.'

'You watering them?'

'Yeah, we water them, daily. We trim the leaves and take care of the weeds. We got it covered, Mum.'

The garden is now a totally different jungle, no longer the playpen of those children, and no longer my mother's masterpiece. It has gone the way of nature, overgrown and grey. There is no colour out there anymore, not in this city anyway. The leaves, the flora, not green but grey. The slabs my father had put down in another of the infinite summers of our youth broken and cracked. A total muddle, a grey wash of everything and anything, one thing barely distinguishable to the next.

I fill the kettle and place it on the stove. The rain sets in on the city, the clouds roll over and the colour fades yet more. I realise, as if anew, that real life is going on out there. Everything inside the house seems suspended, a blur of the same tired moments. On the streets the swathes huddle beneath bus stops and take turns checking their watches. The umbrellas flow like leaves down a river. The kettle sings me back into the kitchen and I lift it off the heat. I take my brother's mug from the sink and shake away the dregs before filling it and placing in the teabag. Slowly stirring I watch as the colour trembles. Lifting the teabag I put it on the hanger above the sticky brown patch on the counter. My brother uses one teabag a day, and we hang that on the peg next to the back door. The peg that Dad used to hang his keys on when he came in. The rattle would let us all know he was back. He is always back now. He stays upstairs in what used to be the spare room. I'm not exactly sure what it is he does up there. Perhaps he dismantles the chapters of his life so far, cuts and pastes, edits out the bad bits, allowing the parts in-between to fall into place. If that is the case then he is still left with the off cuts, the parts he wants to forget, the regrets and the misgivings. I sometimes think of relighting the fire and bringing him down, of leading him past my brother, his son, and to the hearth. It may have been a very long time since he as felt that kind of warmth. I want him to know that it isn't his fault, that we don't blame him. I want this house to be the home that I remember, but deep down I know the most important piece will still be missing.

*

He enters my room on a Saturday like a doctor, his arms full of life. Life that awaits death. Saturday is cemetery day and we go to 'see' or 'visit' Mum. Only it's not *seeing* or *visiting* is it? She is dead. She got ill, we looked after her as best we could, she died, we mourned (we still mourn). But she is still dead. My father has an armful of contradictions, flowers. There are all sorts of flowers, I don't know the names, red and yellow mostly, with a few white wisps of bloom in between. He insists on dressing in a suit and tie, smart in the way that Mum always wanted, smart in the way he never wanted to be. His guilt stretches even to the very clothes he wears. We all have our ways, our little idiosyncrasies, some people call them coping mechanisms, and I guess that Dad's has become this; he does things now that he wished he had done when Mum was still around. I wish he'd done the one thing I think she would have wanted most, to keep the garden splendid. She would much rather an armful of contradictions from the garden than from the city where he got those flowers.

The room was sweltering. She propped herself up and appraised me with pale eyes, her skin like chalk, even the shadows under her eyes the lightest grey.

'You know when I'm gone, I don't want you worshipping my grave like some urchin. Get out and you get on with things okay?' Her voice is a whisper, every syllable croaked out with effort.

'Stop it Mum,' I reply through gritted teeth, nose tingling with the effort of holding back the tears.

'No, I, I can't. We can't keep going on as if this is going to get better. I am going to die.' She's never said that before, no-one has, not even the doctors. I can't remember crying, but I know I must have cried, a lot.

'This was meant to happen, for whatever reason this was what was meant for me honey. When I go then you cry, but not now, not yet.' She reaches out and grasps my hand with what little strength she still has and squeezes it faintly.

'Now tell me, how are the lilies? I had some beautiful ones coming on at the end of the garden.' It's too late for that, the lilies died off months ago, when Mum got really sick. There's nothing out there now, just the stragglers.

'And don't keep coming to the grave, because that won't be me okay? I won't be here anymore.'

I don't tell Dad that bit.

I have just got dressed for the 'visit', suit and tie like always; it's as if we're going to church. A small prayer wouldn't hurt I guess. I hear Dad struggling downstairs.

'Come on now Sandy, on with them please. Please Sandy!' Hurrying downstairs I see him wrestling a pair of trousers onto my brother. He has him propped over his shoulder like some mannequin.

'Dad, Dad, that's no good. Let me help.'

I can tell that he is frustrated, he gets like this. He thinks he can cope with Sandy, but he falters and it gets to him. I lift my brother gently from over his shoulder and sit him back down in his chair. Easily pulling the trousers up to the backs of his legs I lift him just a little and pull them up to his waist.

'Dad, where did you get these, they don't fit.'

'They were in his wardrobe!' My father protests, looking on with frantic eyes.

'Why don't you just throw his old clothes out?' I go over to the chest of drawers in the living room and take out a pair of black trousers that fit his now emaciated figure.

'He's gonna be better before too long I know it, just one day, one step, at a time.' I release an irritated sigh. Going back over to Sandy I pull the trousers onto him and fasten them before turning and taking my father's arm, walking him into the kitchen.

'He's not going to be better before long. People like him don't just recover Dad, it takes years. Sometimes they don't recover at all.
53

So tomorrow we are going to donate his old clothes to charity or something okay?' My dad looks at me wearily, he hasn't got the strength to object. He hasn't even got the resolve to argue now.

'Help me get him into his wheelchair.'

*

'He used to be handsome, didn't he?' She says, standing behind me, her lips almost touching my ear. I lean forward and into my brother's wheelchair, propping myself up by the handles as he stares at the headstone.

'Excuse me?' I look down at my feet, at the spoiled earth and the remnants of snow. I really don't want to be bothered now.

'Your brother, he used to be so handsome.' I turn, face to face with her. A girl, just a few inches smaller than me, arms wrapped around herself, glazed tracks on her cheeks.

'You know my brother?' I ask. She blinks another mascara tear down her face and looks up into the grey sky with her green eyes. Her lips part for a moment, then purse, and then she replies.

'I knew him yeah, a long time ago, I knew him.'

'Sorry, I didn't get your name?' I ask. Her knuckles whiten as she clings more tightly to her slender frame.

'I'm, I'm sorry,' she whispers, turns and begins to walk away. I start and follow, and reach out to grasp her shoulder but stop short.

'Hey, who are you? How do you know my brother?' I ask. She stops, the eaves lean in and hold us in time, stillness descends and we face each other.

'I'm the passenger.' And the moment breaks, the stillness lifts and the air turns colder still. I feel a shudder engage my body and my stomach begins to hurt.

'You're, you're her?' She nods in affirmation, hollowing me out. 'Oh my God, I'm so, so sorry,' is all my lips can frame. She wears the blood in her cheeks like flags, arms wrapped around her stomach now, still in tears.

'You don't need to be sorry, it, it wasn't your fault.' I turn and look to my brother, his jaw slackening in the soft brush of winter light. His frame hunched as he stares, eyes rolling slightly. I realise my breathing is heavy and rushed; I exhale in clumps of air and suck more in as the weight hits me.

'Look, I shouldn't of let him go out that night, he, he'd been on medication, anti-depressants or something. They, they made him

54

drowsy, he couldn't concentrate properly. My dad, he was out at work and I had my mum to look after, I just, I'm just,' My head can't make the sentence, can't make sense of it. I feel the guilt, I feel the press of it in my chest. My heart beats in tribal rhythms as I try to make sense of the encounter. She turns and walks

'I shouldn't have come over, I'm sorry, I just wanted to see him.' she says. I catch up, and walk next to her across the yard. The grass feels strange beneath my feet.

'I wish I could take it back you know, just go back and change everything,' I say. She turns and holds me in her glare, still crying, still wrapped up, her arms taut like elastic bands.

'And you think I don't? You think I don't wake up every morning with a hole here?' She thumps her stomach with a balled fist and barely flinches. 'Right here!' and she continues, thumping her stomach again and again, harder and harder. I grab her arms and force them down to her sides as she thrashes and throws herself away from me, hysterical now with tears, frantic. She lashes herself onto the ground and pulls her knees up to her chest and rocks. I crouch down next to her, and fall onto the ground myself. We sit in silence, for minutes. She cries quietly into herself, and I simply stare at the ground, at the lushness of the ground beneath us, at the fertile earth. More minutes ache by. She plunges her hand into the inside of her coat pocket and conjures a slip of paper, the edges crumpled and stained, she holds it out to me, face still buried into her knees and sobs;

'This is all I have left.' I take the paper, a sonogram. A spider-web mess of white on black, a ghost before it was even born. A nothing. To me. And I realise, that to her, to my brother, this was their everything. This was their present, this was their future and everything they had, every hope crushed into this white shadow. I look at her, at her shuddering body, foetal. This was her, a part of her, a living organ that she failed to protect. That I failed to protect. I turn the sonogram in my hands and find a date on the back. 14/02/2006. The day of the crash. The day I lost a brother. The day my brother lost a son. The day that son lost a grandmother. The day the woman sat next to me lost her youth and her motherhood, and her future, all in a few seconds.

Kate Herbert

The First Cut

Genevieve was perched on a stool ever so slightly higher than the rest of them, she always arranged these get-togethers. Her excitement fizzled like Alka Seltzer in a glass of water and sometimes it hurt Julia's eyes to look at her. Julia kept her shades on and nobody suggested she took them off. She would live in the dark if she could, this whole vampire thing is so now, so sexy, she inhabited the space perfectly. Faye sat on the edge of her seat, her eyes heavily made up, she looked beautifully tragic like a twenties film star.

Genevieve drained her glass, 'God I needed that, it's been one of those days.'

One of those lives more like, thought Faye. Gen refilled their glasses, giggling and spilling a little on her satin blouse. She shuffled in her enormous Mulberry bag and retrieved a packet of fags and waved them at the girls.

'Since when have you been smoking?'

She raised an eyebrow theatrically, 'There's a lot you don't know about me.'

'Clearly,' said Faye.

She hopped off her stool and followed.

She blew a thin plume of smoke that spiralled up over their heads, sensing Faye's eyes on her face, she turned to her friend. 'It's just work, sometimes it's...' She paused and looked as if she might say something, then her eyes landed on some guy. She exhaled dramatically, 'Y'know...' Faye nodded.

'But we're going to have some fun tonight. It's Thursday, officially now part of the weekend,' she announced.

Faye pushed her hands deeper into her pockets, dizzy after a drag, she wasn't a smoker. She'd given up for him, bloody Marcus. She reached for the fag again and steadied herself. She could do what she wanted now. Gen was deep in flirt mode so Faye made her way back to the bar.

Inside the music had got louder, the wine flowed and Faye reapplied her face in the bathroom mirror. She recognised one of the girls who used to work with Marcus and nodded. She slathered on more lippy and walked back through the bar. Julia was hunched over her phone, her face pinched. Faye watched as she rubbed her hands over her eyes beneath her shades. Julia stiffened and looked around the room, composing herself as her friend sat back at the table.

'Everything alright,' Faye asked in a soft voice.

'Fine,' she replied a little too quickly.

Fine... the magnolia paint of words thought Faye.

Julia put on her Versace dark glasses and sat practising her controlled breathing, the EMF technique at £80 per hour, and tried to stop her core from spinning. She can close her eyes behind her bug like frames, that's why she likes them. A Russian doll, that's what Yuri called her and since him there has been no one of any significance. She is closed like the city after dark, she makes cuts in her tiny arms and her skin is pale, like snow on the Russian Steppes. She feels the rain before it pricks her skin and everything is significant and yet she feels so temporary. Looking though her frosted window you would see a young woman, who looks more like a girl, as if she might take to the sky and twist and bend like a runaway kite. The Julia her close friends know is complicated, nobody would deny that, but she is Russian and that seems to explain enough for most. Julia only confides the barest detail and the rest may as well be a state secret. She pulls the cashmere sleeves of her tight jumper to cover her wrists and twists the fabric over her thumbs, she cannot get warm. You should eat something Gen would say, in fact you should eat for a week, then we'll talk, this makes Julia laugh. But she doesn't eat; she keeps her control thermostat on low and survives. The last letter arrived weeks ago, she retrieved it from her bag and re read it.

Why hadn't he called? Julia stared out of the window to the street below, that bloke on the corner again, he gave her the creeps, he doesn't see her, she knew how to keep hidden, and she closed herself like a mussel.

She checked her phone again, even though she hadn't heard the plink it makes when she gets a message, she texted:

I should come home. tell me what to do Jxxx

She stared at the screen, deleted two of the three xs's and pressed send.

She paced, then paused by the cup of cold black coffee on her desk strewn with papers, scribbled in Russian. She scratched her head and put on her heavy fur coat, her glasses and headscarf.

As she exited the apartment, the man flicked his fag to the floor behind him. She walked quickly and the man, even though he had long legs, hurried his pace. She jumped on the bus and headed for town, he jumped in behind. She watched him reflected in the window, her breathing shallow.

The bus stopped and she hurried into John Lewis, she raced for the ladies, pushed the stall door closed behind her and put her head on her knees and breathed. It didn't smell there, a better class of toilet. She removed a tiny case from her pocket and stared at its contents; she picked up a tiny silver blade. Pushing up her sleeve, she held the metal against her pulse and let herself begin to slide. She dragged the blade slowly across her wrist, settling beneath the fold of her elbow and pressed a little harder until small drops of red trickled towards her lap. Staring at the blood, she put the blade away. She wanted to vomit, but knew that feeling would pass, she dropped her head back and the day began to make sense. She applied a plaster also from her pocket and pulled her sleeves low. In the mirror she examined her face. She knew that fear has no place for the brave and she returned to the crowded street. The man was nowhere to be seen. He would find her, they always did.

They paused to look at each other before pushing the door open. Faye held her breath and took a step back as Boris the cat leapt at them.

'No dead body...' said Faye.

'She could just be away,' she said with little conviction as the smell from the perfumed cat litter hit their nostrils. Gen opened the small barred window and the cat slipped out on to the fire escape.

She put the kettle on and they sat at the table, Faye recognised the empty feeling, but it was more than that.

'What are we supposed to do, we're her friends.' They sat in silence, each in their own moment of realisation.

They had waited that night the two of them, sitting in *The Salisbury*, they phoned her several times, but she never answered, she never came.

Faye had noticed her arms once, Julia spilt coffee on her top and she peeled it off and dried herself, she'd laughed but Faye could see it had to hurt; *it's nothing* she had said. Faye saw thin scratches, like pieces of red cotton and pearlescent lines on her white arms. She had tried not to stare, and her mouth opened to say something. Something that was lost when she looked at Julia's face. Their eyes met long enough for her to know to pretend she had seen nothing, perhaps she had imagined the marks, she never mentioned it again.

Faye and Genevieve looked at each other and stood in her room. It was too cold to remove their coats; they fed the cat, waited, paced and then made tea again. They half sat on her ergonomic chairs and looked out of her window above the leafy suburban street, but the man wasn't there anymore, so they never saw what she had seen that day.

The policewoman stood talking into the radio, her hat pulled low over her face partly covered by a port wine birth mark. Gen looked away, rude to stare. But guessed she must be used to that and anyway maybe it wasn't a birthmark but some injury, collateral damage, she looked hard. She took notes and asked a few questions, superficial stuff. Gen wanted to tell her about Julia's laugh, like the sound of a trombone coming from a flute, deep and too big for her tiny frame. Last summer when they'd sat up drinking shots all night, she'd been the one Gen had confided in about her OCD, she hadn't judged. She listened and Gen cried in her arms, she remembered being surprised at Julia's hug; she'd always looked so frail. She hadn't been able to tell Faye who'd had problems finishing a sentence that didn't include the words, Marcus or happy. Faye was happy for her of course, but there was a limit. Looking back that was the biggest joke, what was it her mum always said about appearances? What a mess she thought, shaking her head. But at that moment all she could think about, when she heard her name on the policewoman's lips, was the secrets, just the secrets, but she couldn't say that.

The woman asked if Miss. Rosanov had a partner, her pen poised above the notebook. The girls looked at one another and conversations played out in their heads. They paused, maybe too long; the policewoman tapped her pen and scribbled. They told her there was someone, but that they had never met him, they'd seen him briefly, they coloured in the faint picture as best they could. The PC looked around the flat and talked into her radio, she stood at the door, taking one last look around before leaving.

Faye thought about Marcus and the warmth of their bodies when they had been close together, before. She remembered how much she had loved him, so much it still scratched at the back of her throat when she tried to explain. She had wanted to tell Julia about Marcus. She had tried to talk. But had preferred to drink too much and watch Gen make a fool of herself, better than telly, they had joked. She was close to her friends, when they lived together at University, back then it was better than family. She was lucky to have family, Julia had no one. She'd easily recognised her in the faded Polaroid by her bed. *Is that you*, she'd asked, full of new friendship and interest. You're like your mum, she'd heard herself say. Julia didn't reply she put the photo in the drawer and her back to Faye. When they got to know each other Julia told them about the accident. Faye imagined the car as it burst through the crash barrier and tumbled over and over like a Nana Mouskouri song, over and over and over again. She was cut out of the wreckage, her whole family wiped out, the end. She couldn't imagine waking up and being told the news, when would that ever make any sense thought Faye. Faye had cried and Julia offered her tissues and comfort. She swallowed and put her arms tightly around her body and smiled at Gen as she tried to stop her teeth form chattering.

'I need to get out of here,' Gen put her arm around Faye.

'Drink?' I think we said at the same time.

They took her folder and a few things, and left the coolness of the flat, the window slightly ajar for Boris. They knew it was serious, it's the little things, that's such a cliché, but it's true, hard to explain, the chink of an idea, a suspicion and then all sorts of light filters in. It's like not being aware of a sound until it's pointed out, and you go, oh yeah, I never noticed before and then it's all you can bloody notice. She was gone.

Faye realised she had talked much more to Gen lately, it felt good, like the old days. Gen listened when she talked about Marcus and managed to look interested and concerned in equal measures, for longer than anyone would be expected to do. Faye loved her for that, she needed to just talk. They began to see this other Julia, the bottle of anti-depressants in her room   She wasn't sure why they were so surprised; it was all the rage, wasn't everyone taking happy pills and look at Zeta-Jones, diagnosed bi polar 2, sounded like a sequel to some awful B movie. Faye couldn't sleep that night, restless, alone, post Marcus, bed too big. We spend all our time trying to convince everyone, including ourselves, that everything is *fine*. Well, thought Faye, I have officially abolished that word…It was the last word she said to me and it was a downright lie.

Catherine Hoyle

An Ecstasy of Fumbling

A safety pin holds the crimson paper to her coat, fastened expertly by her father that morning.

'Do you know what this is Catie?'

The girl shrugged and shuffled her feet, mumbling 'Flower' before looking upward with grey-gold eyes. He had smiled briefly, prompting, 'What sort of flower?'

Before the feet shuffled once more and she examined him, looking for the answer...

'Red?'

The 'R' was rolled and the 'D' elongated so the word sounded 'rrrred-uh'. He had sighed slightly and knelt down to Catie's height.

'You know how your Nan likes to talk about the war?'

'Where Bampa saved us from the bad guys?'

Fumble. He glances up and around the room.

'What do you mean 'bad guys', Bach?'

Her hand fiddles with a toggle. Hesitantly...

'Nan says they killed lots of people and Bampa tried to make them stop.'

Just leave it. She's too young.

'Okay...Well, a lot of people were killed on both sides and they weren't all bad guys. They had families and children and grandchildren and...'

He pauses and takes a deep breath, leaning back on his hands.

'These flowers are poppies and we wear them to remember everyone that shouldn't have died in war times.'

The blonde brow is furrowed but she remains silent.

The room is full of bright purple kinetic energy. Bouncing from the light fittings, off the T-Bars, off the barmaids' faces. This is my 7th pint of Guinness and my hat is a green shamrock – raising my height by an extra foot.

Looking up at the light fittings and away.

Sway.

The light trails and tries to follow as I move my head around. The first time I saw a shooting star was with you. We made wishes.

Remember?
I just want to be happy –You could make me happy – You did – We were.
'What did you wish?' You had smiled.
Pause.
'If I tell you it won't come true' had been my coy reply, and it did come true. We were.
We were soldiers…Soldiers, bombs, guns, The Cranberries, remember that song? Our song.

'Another mother's breaking heart is taking over. When the violence causes silence, we must be…..Mistaken? Mistaking?'

We always argued over that word… I still don't know the answer. If you were here now I would just agree with you. I would. But you wouldn't believe me.
I don't know what happened… We were happy.
I wonder if my blood is black. Eight pints of Guinness now. Aren't there eight pints of blood in the body?
Pints of blood, organs, brains, pieces…Flown back to us in pieces.
If I could do it all again it would all be different.
People are blissfully jigging through the energy – the fiddle notes materialise, catch the purple haze and float about my head. Mosquitoes. I bat them away, and again, I sway.

Catie holds tightly onto her father's trouser leg as they walk through the town square. There are people everywhere. They stop after what feels like miles at the statue in the square.
'Cenotaph, not statue, Bach.'
'Oh...'
Her father lifts her onto his shoulders, pulling her from the sea of legs. There are boys about her cousin's age in camouflage and the same crimson paper catches her gaze from every angle.
The sea is calm and quiet. Somebody is speaking but the wind catches their words and blows them where Catie can't hear.
'After the bugle, you need to be silent until I say so Catie, okay?'
She nods, eyes fixed on the uniformed men, stood stiller than anything she has ever seen.

You gave me butterflies the first time I saw you in uniform. I think I was proud – A ridiculous concept now, I know.

Remember when we first held hands? It was freezing cold and those same butterflies exploded at your touch.
Exploded.
Shudder.
It's been fourteen months – I'm still waiting. If you can hear me now I'm in the purple mist next to the crotchets and treble clefs.
I'll wait – you'll come – you wouldn't leave me here.
You promised.
If I had my wish again we both know I would change it. Would you?
I spend hours in dark fields, waiting. If I can find the right star maybe I could change this. 'Cos I would give anything to wake up next to you for one more day, to hear you snore or talk in your sleep.
The purple energy clouds over, dulled suddenly around me. It's more of a browny-grey now.
I never believed in this fucking war. I should have walked away. I always knew this could happen and like a fool I stayed with you... We were happy.

A bugler begins to play and Catie frowns. She thinks of the Bampa she never got to meet and about her Nan making bombs and the scars hidden on her wrinkled hands. No-one speaks. The lady next to them is dabbing her face with a handkerchief. Catie tries to smile at her but everybody is looking down.

'I'll see you soon, take care of yourself – I love you.'
You went and you left me.
'I will. I promise.'
I am the walking wounded. Tenth pint of anaesthetic Guinness.
We were happy.
I hope the old lie sits well on your conscience. Beautifully said, Wilfred me old matey.
I should have never let you go... But you promised me.
Tenth pint – down in one.
I sway.
A treble clef hits me between my eyes. Stumble. Oak floor.
And I'm away.

Glancing at the...the...Cenotaph? Lots of poppies have appeared. How?

Brass rings through the air once more and that same voice floats past her on the wind.

Sam Harman

Bugs

'Uh, yeah, we, uh, found her near the corner of, uh, 53rd & 3rd, sitting in a doorway. She, uh, she… Well, she didn't seem to know, like, where she was. To be honest, uh, she wasn't even really speaking, just, uh, moaning and giggling and sobbing. Although, after a while, like, I'm sure I could make out her saying the word 'again' over and over and over. It was, uh, really freaky, y'know?'

'No, her… Her skin was like that when we found her. My girlfriend had to run off and, uh, y'know, puke? We kind of think it looks like the girl, y'know, did it to, uh, herself. When we found her, she was, like, just clawing and scraping at her skin. It was fucking gross, man!! There were just clumps of, uh, bloody skin, all around her. And under her fingernails. It looked like she'd tried to fuck a sheet of barbed wire or something. To be, honest, I nearly, like, puked. She'd done it to her face, legs, stomach, everything.'

'Do you reckon she had anything under her skin? 'Cos that's all we could think. Or she spilt something on herself, I dunno. For a nut-sack, though, she was wearing what looked like real expensive clothes. She, uh, looked like she'd been out on the town or something.'

'Maybe she'd, y'know, been to one of those drug parties those rich yuppie-type people have. Maybe, I dunno, 'dropped' something she shouldn't have. Bad LSD trip? I dunno, could be. Maybe PCP or some shit. Anyways, I hope she, uh, gets taken care of. Which hospital is she going to? We might, y'know, check up on her, she looks like she could need, like, someone to watch out for her…'

*

'Are you ready yet?' he heard her moan from the other room. Tonight was the night. He reached into the bathroom cabinet and took out a jar. Within the jar was the body of a fair-sized house spider he'd recently trapped and saved just for this very moment. It had to be bigger than average, otherwise she wouldn't freak out as much. Unscrewing the jar and tipping the contents into the sink, he began to cough loudly. Spitting on the deceased spider for good measure (and don't forget realism), he murmured:

'Uh, babes, come here, would you? I just coughed something up, and, well, I'm pretty scared…' She sighed, rose and walked casually to the bathroom.

'What is it now?' she sighed, not wanting (but expecting) another one of his practical jokes. She was well aware of his irritating mischievous side; but the spider in a puddle of dribble and the (fake) look of worry on his face caught her off guard. She cried out, shivered, and then screamed as the image of the dead spider took up residence in her mind. She'd always been terrified of insects and the like, although she didn't hate them, they just always seemed to target her as the one to sting. To scratch and bite, to crawl over. As she began to spin around on the spot and moan, he couldn't hold the laughter in anymore. *Her face!* was all he kept thinking, as he struggled to stay upright, his body wracked with the spasms of a cruel joke that's gone flawlessly. She stormed over to him and punched him on the shoulder with all the strength she could use.

'You're such a prick!! You know I hate them, you suck-ass piece of shit! Why the fuck would you do that, hey? Hey?' her voice shrill and wavering. His face red, as if all the blood in his body was being forced up his neck, he spluttered:

'But seriously, the look on your *face*!! I'm *so* sorry, but I had to do it' and grinned. She was pretty sure that she would never leave him, no matter the stupid shit he pulled, as long as he just kept grinning like that. It made her tingle.

'Well, stop being an ass, get rid of that horrible fucking thing, and get ready, for god's sake! We have to leave in twenty. They won't like being stood up.' She narrowed her eyes, but couldn't hold it for long. Smiling slightly, she went back to the sitting room and poured another glass of wine.

*

'OK, keys, wallet, bank card, cocaine' he winked at her, patting down his pockets, 'All good to go here.'

'Thank Christ for that' she groaned. They were already late as it was.

He moved his hand up to his face and coughed.

And coughed again.

This time he felt something on his fingers. Casting his eyes downward at his hand, it appeared that a large spider was twitching across it.

'What is it?' she asked, noting the changed expression on his face.

'Nothing, nothing.' He made to shake it off his hand, but another wracking cough went through him. This time he felt *things* moving on his tongue and lips, before feeling those same things fall onto his hand. Not wanting to look (but having to, nonetheless), beetles of various hues and species that had landed on his hand were attacking the spider. He stared open-mouthed at his bug-lined appendage, a sick sense of unease spreading through him like a virus.

'Are those...? What the fuck is going on?' She sounded close to breaking.

'I don't know!! I don't feel very –' he began, then a jet of insects came pouring from his throat. He could feel them crawling over his teeth, around his face. Could feel them writhing around the back of his eyes, looking for escape, itching all under his skin. Only, this wasn't itching, it was torture. By now, doubled up on the floor, the tiny creatures streamed from his nose and ears. He could feel them probing around his stomach, his entire insides. She couldn't handle it any longer and fled from the apartment, screaming no words, just child-like sounds. At this point, he was virtually the last thing on her mind.

Contemplating pulling out his own eyes to ease the scratching behind them, he took one last glance around and thought. As scared as he was, as frightened and disgusted as he was, he couldn't help but admire the bizarre beauty in front of him. Thousands upon thousands of tiny bugs, uncountable different colours, species and sizes, all running around on his sterile white apartment floor. Like the floor of a jungle. With that thought, he slumped forward and died.

*

The green canopy of trees is incredibly dense, but every now and then a spear of sunlight appears to prop it up. Dust motes, picked out in sharp detail glide through the too-yellow light. Trees and trees and trees, vines hanging and wrapped. Strange plants, strange flowers. The jungle is the most beautiful thing you have ever experienced. At eight years old, the temptation to simply run from the safety of your parents and have an adventure is almost too overwhelming, but for the time being you stay put.

She notices the noise. So many living things, animals, bugs, birds, all attempting to out-do each other with the sheer volume of their calls. Chirping, rattling, barking, squeaking, clicking, groaning, rustling; she was glad that she was staying in a hotel a few miles from this part of the jungle, all that noise at night would be enough to drive her crazy-mad.

There are so many sights and sounds (and smells) to take in at once. You have never seen so many exotic colours at the same time; it's beautiful. For the first time ever, you can't wait to return to school and tell everyone about it and draw pictures of it and try to make the animal sounds you hear now and make all the other kids jealous. You turn to thank your parents for letting you come with them and their friends on this expedition, but they have moved off, gone to examine a tree, which to your young mind looks at least twice as big and wide as those skyscrapers you saw once in... Well, you'll remember where it was some other time.

She notices the sound of water coming from very close by. She closes her eyes, becomes very still, listening. Inclining her head slightly to the right, she opens her eyes and walks in the direction of the sound. After thirty seconds or so, she comes across a pretty little ribbon of a stream. Along the banks are odd mounds of earth, like the moles make back home, but much bigger, reaching up to her waist. It is then that she realises that the sound wasn't only water rushing, but thousands upon thousands of tiny insect clicks. Her skin pops out in goose bumps for a moment. But, the feeling passes, and she timidly steps closer.

You can smell an odd musk hanging in the air; sweet, but a little like bad food, like when the cooks at school mess up dinner. You look around, just to check you can still see your parents, and there, tiny in the distance through the leaves and vines, you can make out your dad's yellow sweater tied round his waist. Good. Well, if anything happens, they're not too far away. It's then that your childish mind does what any kid would do in your position, which is to poke at the nearest earth-mound with a stick.

She notices a longish stick a little further up the stream. As she carefully steps towards it, the moist soil on the bank of the stream picks this moment to give way. First, she feels her balance shifting. Then her arms begin to flail. She utters a little yelp as she finally ends up, face-first, into the closest earth-mound. It is then that she feels the vibration of a million tiny feet marching in her direction. Thousands upon thousands of tiny bugs, uncountable different colours, species and sizes march out of the mounds to defend their home against this giant intruder. Fear, of a kind that she will only ever experience once more in her life, paralyses her completely, not even a whimper making it out of her mouth...

67

A. Owen James

8

It was Monday when my father emailed me asking if I could come up to Cheltenham to a party he has organised to celebrate his retirement. The email was polite and said it would be on Wednesday at AreaEight Bar (which I've never been to) – also adding that if I wanted to bring a date for the night that would be fine. I decide not to email back but I do head the train station to buy tickets in advance.

I arrive early at the station and I get the five twenty eight out to Cheltenham and it's only once I'm sat down and the train is pulling out of the station I realise that I didn't invite anyone else up with me – though if I had asked Jessica she would have said no and if I had asked Andi or Sue they would have most likely been busy.

The journey doesn't take long but I forget to bring anything with me – no book, music or anything so I spend most of the time looking out of the window or staring at a woman a few seats down from me. The child with her keeps crying but she doesn't even look at it and by the end of the journey I am very close to shouting at the child myself.

From the train station I order a cab to AreaEight and for a little while the taxi driver looked confused about where I was asking to go. I tell him again and he nods and starts driving. As he pulls out into the road I see the child from the train walking out of the station by himself and he looks no older than eight.

When I arrive at the bar I'm struck by how nice the place is. The name of the bar written on a huge metallic sign above the entrance and the interior looks chic and stylish. As I enter through the heavy glass doors I scan across the room and try and find my father's face within the crowds of people.

He had worked at the power company for what must have been over twenty years and looking across the room I can see plenty of people that certainly look like co-workers – all dressed in the same bland sort of way that my father did – all standing in little circles leaning into one another's ears to talk and all looking tired and kind of overworked.

I see my father from across the room and he's talking to a couple of guys that I don't recognise (but why would I) so I make my way over to him. I tap him on the shoulder and he turns around quickly, cutting off the conversation he was having with the two other men and he looks genuinely pleased to see me. He shakes my hand and tries to give me a sort of hug but because he's holding an almost full drink there is little effort in it and he only uses one arm.

'Nice place here, Dad.'

'You like?' He looks pleased with himself 'Henry, this is Ken and Pete' gesturing at the two men – I nod and they nod back. 'So how have you been?'

'Good' I tell him. We talk a little while about a few things and I ask him how long he's been organising this party for. He tells me but I can't quite hear over the music but I nod. I tell him that I need to buy him a drink but he tells me to wait.

'Mum here?' I ask in a moment of silence between us. I don't think he hears me so I ask again.

'I didn't think she'd want to come.' He tells me.

'You didn't ask her?'

'No.' He breaks. 'She's probably not even here anyway. I think a while ago she said she was planning on moving. Did she tell you anything about that?'

I tell him no and he looks even more disappointed so I ask him what he wants to drink. He tells me a whiskey and I move to the bar. The place is quite crowded and it's coming up to nine. I pull myself up against the bar and look at the huge round mirror that hangs on the wall behind the bottles. It looks kind of unsteady like it could fall. The barman is still busy serving other people so I look around me. As I turn to my left the man who was standing directly next to me moves with his drinks and walks away. Behind him (and now standing closer to me) is a girl – she looks back at me and smiles.

She's wearing a short flowery dress that covers only half of her thigh. Her brown hair is cut short on the sides and back, and her fringe hangs over one side of her face. Her lips are red with lipstick and her face is clear and blushed. I smile back at her and she turns away. I look around again and see where the barman is, but he's still serving someone else. I look back to the girl and as she turns – showing different angles of her face – I notice how young she looks. She could pass for sixteen and I look at the rest of her. Her breasts are small and firm looking, legs waxed but shaded by the bar and her

69

hands frail and perfect. She sees that I'm looking at her again – and again she smiles.

'Hello' she says quietly into my ear. She's moved closer to me while I was ordering my drinks, and I turn to look at her face.

'Hello' I don't know why but I hold out my hand – she takes it delicately and gives a little shake – my fingers wrapped around hers. 'I'm Henry.'

'Lizzy' She smiles again showing beautiful white teeth and I wonder if I should ask if she wants a drink. She's in here so it's likely that she's old enough – and even if she isn't she'll probably say yes anyway. 'Nice to meet you Henry. I like your Jacket.'

'Thanks – Liz or Lizzy?'

'Lizzy I guess. You a student here?' She asks sweetly, I don't offer her a drink but mine come and I notice she doesn't have one. I tell her no and that I'm a teacher. She asks where I'm from and I tell her.

'You from Cheltenham?' I ask her.

'No, I'm just studying here. I'm from London.'

'What are you studying?' I take a sip of my vodka and realise I need a cigarette. I keep looking her over and she knows this and her small breasts are almost pushing up against my arm now.

'Sociology, Maths and English' she smiles 'It's fun.'

I ask her how she is doing all three –

'You said you were a student?'

'I am. I'm in college.'

'But you were said you were down from London?' I ask her.

'Yeah, me and my mum moved down here a few years ago.' She tells me still smiling.

'How old are you then?' As I ask this I wish I hadn't but she is very pretty and I want to know.

'I'm sixteen.' Resting her arm on the bar – maybe trying to look older or more relaxed in this environment.

I look over her again and she smiles. I smile back and nod as if to validate her.

'How old are you?'

I tell her and she asks where I teach. My father's whiskey is set down upon the bar next to my drink and I hand the barman a ten pounds note.

'Well I'm not quite a teacher. It's in Cardiff' – I pause – 'I'm an actor really – well kind of – but I teach acting – in Novel.' She looks

70

at me blankly 'Have you heard of it?' As I ask I lean in towards her ear – thinking maybe she just didn't hear me first of all.

'No. I haven't. Sounds cool though.'

I ask her who she's here with and she tells me her mum and I nod.

'You hang around a lot with your mum?' I ask wondering how old her mother might be. She nods and I ask her how come they're both here tonight.

'A party or something. My mum's here with a few people – I just wanted to leave the house and do something. She asked and I said yes.' Her smile fades for a moment and then returns.

'Where is she?'

She points her out from across the room. She points to quite a pretty woman of about forty wearing a dark dress with her hair pinned back loosely.

I ask her – 'That woman there? In the black?' and she nods. The woman she pointed at is standing next to my father and the two are standing closely together and talking to each other, each moving into to the other's ears as they speak and then leaning back.

'What's her name?'

'Claire.'

'Do those two know each other?' I ask her, pointing at her mother and my father. 'You know that guy?'

'That's her boyfriend – partner – whatever. It's his retirement or something. That's why I'm here.' She shrugs and I look back over to my father and Claire.

'That's my dad she's with. He invited me up the other day.' I pause for a moment and Lizzy looks back at me – beautiful but without her smile. 'I didn't know he was with anyone.' I tell her and she looks back blankly. We both look over at the two and they look back. My father raises his glass to me and Claire waves to Lizzy. I nod back and Lizzy waves.

'Does that mean we are brother and sister?' she asks after a little while. I shake my head and ask if she wants a drink. She says no and then yes, so I buy her a Bacardi and coke. When It arrives I hand it to her and the barman looks at me suspiciously as I hand him the money. I walk over to my father and Claire – hand him his drink and smile at Claire.

I turn back to look at the bar and Lizzy is sat sipping her drink looking into the huge round mirror smiling. The space at the bar where I had been remains empty.

After a few more drinks and introductions to people I will never meet again my father asks me where I am staying tonight. I realise that I didn't make any plans and perhaps I had kind of assumed that I would be staying at my father's house. He tells me that Claire is staying around his house tonight and that Lizzy is too.

'You going to stay around mine tonight then?' he asks with a prominent slur.

'Yeah I guess.'

He motions to the bar with his empty glass and asks what I want to drink. I tell him that I'll have a vodka and orange and he nods. It's almost midnight now according to my watch and I look around trying to find Claire wondering if she's driving.

I see both her and Lizzy stood at the end of the bar with a couple of other women. They both look slightly bored and I can't tell if Claire is holding a drink – but I can see that Lizzy is. As I follow my father towards the bar, Lizzy looks over and nods, taking a sip of her drink. (I think how similar they look – I wonder if I find Claire attractive too, and if I do, is that because of her daughter.) Just as I approach the bar Lizzy leans down stretching her rear out and (just for a second) I stop to look.

Like I thought, Claire ends up driving – I think she's tipsy but I don't worry and neither does anyone else. When the four of us arrive back at my father's house it is almost one in the morning and Claire has to help my father out of the passenger seat and leads him up to the front door. I don't know how many drinks he's had throughout the night but I don't think he could have had much more than me. Once inside my father settles on one of the stools in the kitchen - for a moment Claire, Lizzy and I watch him before taking seats ourselves.

We all talk for a little while about the night which wasn't particularly interesting before my father stands and fetches a bottle of whiskey and four glasses from one of the cabinets. He pours us all a drink each and takes a heavy swig from his glass.

Lizzy moves to the fridge and pulls out a bottle of orange juice as me and Claire sip our glasses – watching her slightly from the corner of my eye she moves delicately around the room. We talk for a little while and my father has several more drinks – and when he starts hiccupping Claire suggests that they go to bed.

As she helps him up she says goodnight to both me and Lizzy.

'The spare room next to Lizzy's is yours, mate.' My father tells me as he struggles out of the room. They both say goodnight and I pour myself another drink as they head upstairs. I wish he didn't call me mate but I can't help but laugh at this point and so does Lizzy. We look at each other, both laughing and she takes another sip from her orange juice.

She stands after a little while and moves to the sofa in the front room and I follow her.

'Did you want your drink?' I ask as I stand in the doorway between the two rooms. The juice is gone but the whiskey still sits on the table.

She shakes her head as she walks and I notice how unsteady she seems now and I wonder how many drinks she has had while out. I think I bought her at least two during the night – both times Bacardi and coke, but I can't remember if they were singles or doubles.

We sit next to each other on the cool leather sofa and she picks up the remote from the coffee table and flicks channels until she stops on some sort of nature documentary.

'Do you like these kinds of programmes?' I ask her smiling – almost laughing at her choice of late night programming.

'Yeah sometimes,' she says wedging herself further into the sofa, curling up. 'You're nice Henry.'

'Thanks.'

She moves over closer to me and lays her head down on my shoulder and I can't tell if she has closed her eyes, so I ask her if she is tired. She tells me no and then talks for several minutes about the reasons she likes wildlife documentaries – as she does my eyes feel like they are glazing over as I stare into the television screen but I try and listen to at least some of what she is saying.

I tell her I'm not too keen on them once I think she has finished – she then looks up at me – our faces close – and tells me she just finds them relaxing, then replaces her head back to my shoulder.

We talk for a little longer and I still don't know if her eyes are open. Then I feel her hand on my leg and I can feel it moving up my thigh. I look down at her legs and I can see that her skirt has moved up her legs and if it were to move any higher I would be able to see her underwear.

'I really like you Henry' she tells me as she looks back up – our faces almost touching. She looks into my eyes as her hand lands on my crotch and she feels my erection. She smiles and lets out a little laugh as she moves in to kiss me.

I come hard inside of her and she pants heavily (almost grunting) as I slowly stop thrusting. Immediately after I roll off her onto the other side of the bed, panic strikes as I worry that either Claire or my father might have heard, but when I realise there is nothing I can do now I calm down. I glance across from the ceiling towards Lizzy and my eyes follow her arms down to her crotch to see that she is still touching herself – so I look for my cigarettes.

I wake up in the spare room and say goodbye to my father and Claire before I leave. They ask me why I'm going so early and I tell them it's past noon and I need to get back to my classes.

My train arrives on time and the carriage I get onto is completely empty and I manage to masturbate twice before we arrive at the next stop where a boy of about fifteen gets on. He's wearing dark sunglasses even though it's cloudy outside and I'm pretty sure he keeps looking at me.

Alex Trew

The Day the Cows Came Home

Little Bickerton is a small village set in the south of England like a pearl in a pearl necklace. It has a post office and a petrol station and a local shop where the residents can buy whatever they may need; from the *Bickerton Bugle* to a pot of pure honey from Ida Jenkins' Bee Barn, two pounds a pot, five for a jar. Like many small towns, Little Bickerton has one main road running through it, the big tarmac vein that branches off into little capillaries, the smaller roads that lead into the mid-Seventies estate in the north of the town. Here you can find white trapezoid homes, complete with thin panels of painted wood stuck to the front like posters on a child's bedroom wall. Dozens of Volvos and Mini Coopers are parked in the streets.

Follow this road in the opposite direction – to the south – and you reach what some of the older residents dub 'the heart of Bick'. Here, low walls of stone and granite blocks separate the vast ivy-choked houses from one another. Every property has an ornate gate, messy with excessive design, and long driveways paved like the streets of Paris, scrubbed gargoyles on the lawns, forever vomiting glassy water into the Koi ponds.

It is in this part of Little Bickerton Harry York lives with his wife Diane and their two young daughters, Rose and baby Leila. Harry is Little Bickerton's Mayor; five months into his first term after toppling the twenty six-year incumbent Herbie Mackintosh in the most closely fought election campaign seen in the town for more than a decade. Before he was mayor, Harry was a field medic in Iraq, serving three tours of duty from 2003 onwards.

Diane, an American originally hailing from Arizona, is an author and is currently writing her third novel; set in the Wild West, it follows two brothers as they search for the murderer of their mother. The killer is eventually revealed as their estranged father. Diane is having an on-off affair with a woman named Elena, sous chef at the family's favourite restaurant. She wants to return to the States once Harry's term is up.

Their eldest daughter, Rose, is nine years old and has a special kind of loathing for her new sister. Most days after school finishes, she throws pebbles at the trees in the woods just behind her house, another ivy-clad Georgian mansion located atop a small hill just above the town.

They should love me most; I'm the bloody oldest. Why the bloody hell did they even have Leila? Nobody bloody asked me. Rose had recently picked up on one of her father's favourite words, much to her mother's despair. I hate that bloody baby.

When relatives come over to grin and gurn over Leila, Rose throws her arms to her sides and storms out of the room, huffing and puffing like an old steam train up to her bedroom.

Ignore her. Sibling jealousy isn't it.

Oh yes, our James was quite the same when Max was born. They all get over it after a while.

Rose looks out of her bedroom window at the town below. People as small as woodlice were scuttling in and out of tiny woodlice buildings, shopping for carrots and turnips and talking to one another about nothing at all. Outside of town itself were acres and acres of fields; long grass woven with faded greens and washed-out yellows; muddy soil, all churned-up post-harvest; fields dotted with cows and sheep like the night sky is dotted with shining stars. Beyond, the waning sunlight shatters into a million tiny shards on the horizon and Rose York cries like a little girl.

Then one hot summer's night, Rose is awoken by loud noises coming from outside her bedroom window. She had been sent to bed early so her parents could shout at one another but that had been hours ago. The alien, pale green glow from her alarm clock read 01:49am. She lays hugging the covers, listening out for the slightest creaking floorboard or dropping pin. Another *thud*, something hitting metal with a grunt. Rose lowers one foot to the floor, followed by the other; somewhat calmed by the feeling of the shag rug between her toes. There was a tiny crack in her curtains, and a thin icicle of moonlight stretched all the way from the window to her feet, turning them a ghostly white. Like a hunter stalking his prey through still woodland, Rose pads across her room, deftly placing one foot before the other, avoiding the toy clown fish and Barbies strewn like landmines in the dark.

She reaches the curtains and hesitates. Turning, Rose looks at her bed and at the closed door to her bedroom and then she turns back to the window. Yet another *thud* and a deep grunt from outside. Her hand trembles before her eyes as it opens the crack of light, the spectral glow of the moonbeam creeping wider and wider across her face as she exposes the twilight world beyond the glass. There are big black shapes moving around the garden and between the Range Rovers on the gravelled driveway below her window. Her skin freezes and it takes Rose a few moments to realize that the things stumbling and bumbling in the dark, knocking into the cars and flowerpots are cows. This has happened a few times before. Mr Owens, the farmer who owns the land next to the York house is notoriously lax in ensuring that his cattle stay within the confines of their fields.

For a long time, Rose watches the cows chew on the hedges and she chuckles as one wades through the pond where her fairies live. In the morning, her mother finds her sleeping at the foot of the windowsill.

That morning, the streets of Little Bickerton are deadlocked with traffic. No-one is moving an inch for the cows. There are hundreds of them, just standing there in the road, on the pavements, in people's gardens, staring at the ground, staring at the sky, eating shrubbery, walking into cars. Some residents, particularly those with cows on their property, shout and gesticulate into their telephones, red-faced and sweaty in their dressing gowns. Mr Owens is outside the village hall, trying in vain to round up the cows that belong to him. According to the policemen patrolling the town, the cows had deserted the fields and moved in during the night but they could offer no explanation why.

Harry sits in his office, mug of cold coffee and a half-eaten bacon sandwich on his desk, calling every farmer in a twenty-mile radius, informing those that don't already know that their animals are invading Little Bickerton. His assistants flit back and forth around him like moths.

Rose and all the children her age have been turned away from school: Mr Owens' bull – nicknamed Ali – is circling the playground, snorting and dribbling, charging at the swings and slides, shattering the scratched yellow plastic with his huge horns.

I'm always telling that bloody fool, he needs to put fence around his land. At least put that monster in a pen, for God's sake. This is a joke, said Dr Davies, the school's headmaster, standing on the street side of the playground wall.

He does, Mike. I was just talking to him; he says the gate was in splinters when he went to feed the chickens this morning. Only twenty or so of these are his, y'know, replied Mrs Bernard, the deputy.

A bloody joke.

Diane takes Rose and her best friend, Laura Lewis, to the Jolly Griffin Coffee Shop for cans of coke and shortbread on a plate. Baby Leila is staying with her grandparents. The girls ask her why the cows are everywhere. She looks up from her BlackBerry and tells them it was because the god of the cows is pissed off with them all for eating so much McDonalds.

We learned about the cow goddess in school. Mr Thomas says that she's Egyptian.

Yeah, well she's really pissed at us. Her phone lights up and vibrates across the table. Hello, Elena. Stay here you two. Rose and Laura watch her through the plate glass window, walking alongside the cows in the road, grinning as she speaks. The girls talk about the cow goddess for a while. Laura tells Rose they should play in the fields seeing as they're empty. Rose says they should wait for her mum to get back.

Three RSPCA vans arrive a little after lunch. The men and women in the blue uniforms disappear to talk with the bemused and helpless farmers. The number of cows seems to be constantly growing; there is less and less space to walk between them. Under the burning summer sun, the warm and ripe stench of the cows is overwhelming; those who have not yet returned to their homes wear handkerchiefs held over the faces.

The cows would not budge an inch, mooing long into the night.

For three days Little Bickerton was overrun. By the second afternoon the smell of urine and faeces and sweat was so strong, the police advised all inhabitants to remain indoors with the windows shut. Whilst playing with her dog, Rusty the German Shepherd, Rose overheard her father telling her mother that there had been a number of accidents on the back roads that led to town and to the coast; people crashing straight into a lone cow hidden around a blind corner or careening into a small herd in the middle of the night.

So far there have been nine cow-related injuries and two deaths. Two people have died because of these bloody cows. Apparently we're living inside a fucking cartoon.

The cows' behaviour was strange. They were beginning to force their way into people's homes. First, an inquisitive individual would sniff a door or window, licking it or staring inside through the glass. Then more would do the same, crowding the front lawns and driveways before forcibly pushing themselves through the door to the horror of those inside. Mrs Barnes, an octogenarian who lived alone in a three-storey mansion on Turnbull Lane, was awoken at five in the morning by a calf licking her face, its mother chewing on her bed sheets.

The media arrived and made short films that made the evening news across all the big channels. A journalist interviewed Harry and the story was published on page seventeen in *The Sun* the next day under the headline: 'The Day the Cows Came Home'. The town became a national joke, people driving across the country to see the 'Cow Town'.

And then they left. On the night of the third day, a few of the stragglers on the outskirts began to wander off, some to the fields, some down the country lanes or into the woods. Slowly, the rest began to follow; leaving gardens and driveways, vacating the village square, filtering off into the countryside like ants following the path of a dried-up riverbed.

Rose watched the exodus from her bedroom window and was sad that the cows were going. Below, her mother ran out onto the driveway and threw her phone to the ground, stamped on it, and drove away in her car.

Sonnie Hazell Wills

Through The Flames

She's breathing hard. Filled with adrenaline. Her breasts rise and sink rapidly. Her heart beats so fast I can see it making the skin on her chest quiver. I've never seen that look in her eyes before. Blazing bright and fierce, shimmering almost. She is beautiful. Wild. I want to take her outside. As though I know she belongs there.

This change in her is striking. I know every freckle on her skin, every scar and blemish. Yet it's like I'm looking at her anew.

I can't stop staring.

Her tongue teases her lips, licking some of the red off which speckles her face. I can feel my pulse getting harder. I brush a strand of hair away from her eyes.

-You look beautiful.

She snaps her gaze to mine and I feel my body setting alight. She smiles. The smile a tiger would give you, before it rips you limb from limb. She moves towards me and kisses me hard. Her lips taste like copper. I bite them. She whimpers. She knows I like that.

–Take off your dress.

She gives me the same hard smile and slips it off her shoulders. Letting it drop to her feet. My eyes roam all over her creamy skin. Here and there, mainly on her face, it's spotted. With specks of red. Fresh, wet red. It burns in the twilight of the room. I look for the perfect place.

–Your ribs.

She nods and lifts up her left arm, baring her side to me. I feel the blade in my fingers. I wipe it clean. It seems extravagant for her thin skin. I put my hands on her sparrow frame and push the blade, ever so gently, into her skin. Deep enough to scar, no further. It feels like little more than a membrane. She bites her lip but doesn't blink. I score a line, following the shape of her rib and after a moment, a small crimson thread blossoms along the slit. Barely there.

–Number one. That's all we need. Until next time.

I kiss her. She smiles and puts her arm down. Rather than reaching for her dress, she moves to the window and stares through the gap in the long curtains.

She always stares. Never just glances. Like she is trying to burn the image she sees.

The chink in the curtains lets the sunlight in. The slant of light illuminates the dust in the air. Swirling like petrol on water. I wonder why it hasn't settled yet. There is so much of it. It's always there. Only visible when the sun is at that perfect angle. It shows the dust hanging in the air like glitter.

– Come away from there.

She begins to walk backwards. Smiling at me. She reaches the bed and sits down. She looks so simple and fierce in these rich surroundings. A warrior woman. Flecked with blood.

–What are you doing?

She reaches behind her and pulls her bra off of her pale shoulders, and lets it fall to the floor. Rose bud nipples for my eyes. Only mine. I want to touch them. She wants me to. So I won't. I can feel myself smiling. I pull my tie off and hold it limp in my hand.

–Are you flirting with me?

Her smile broadens. She leans back onto her elbows and opens her legs. My breathing is suddenly becoming a conscious effort. Harder. She thumbs the waistband of her cotton underwear.

- Show me.

She pulls the crotch to one side and lets me stare. I can feel life throbbing in my chest.

–You look like a whore.

She smiles and pushes her fingers inside herself. I'm starting to tremble. I start towards her and grab a handful of her hair.

– Who is this for?

– You.

I can smell her hot sweet breath. She's not afraid of me. Not right now. I let go and stand back. She slips off her underwear and drops it to the floor. She leans back again and opens her legs wider. She knows I like that.

My eyes touch all of her body. Ivory, melting into peach, fading into deep pink. And here and there, speckled with foreign scarlet. I find it amazing that the more concealed and more intimate a place on her body, the more vibrant it appears.

I take off my trousers. Folding them and placing them next to the jacket. Even though I know I'm going to burn them later. I unbutton my shirt one by one. I won't rush for her. She's fingering the cut on her ribs. Smudging the congealing blood.

81

– Leave it.

I pull her legs around my waist and she whimpers.

So much skin.

Hers, nearly translucent it's so pale. My hands gripping her thighs look caramel in comparison. It all melts together.

No. Too nice. I pull away and flip her onto her stomach. Everything is rougher, tougher, louder, sweatier. My grip gets tighter on her hips. My fingers dig into her skin making it swell around each digit.

– You're hurting me.

– Good girl.

She knows what I want to hear.

Everything is sparking. Lighting the fuse. I feel it. As it's burning shorter and shorter. My muscles tighten and she feels it. Her skin is going to bruise.

I collapse onto her back.

She lies beneath me panting. I kiss the back of her head. Her voice is muffled.

– I love you.

– I love you too.

We stay there for a moment. Or an hour. Soaking the film of sweat off of each other's bodies. I feel her heartbeat through her back, almost as though it's trying to punch in time to mine. My breath moves her hair. Even now, after, every movement my body makes, hers has a reaction to.

I roll onto the sheets. Silky and smooth, they stick to my skin. Such a tacky gold colour. A gold I didn't want. But it looked expensive. The gold is splashed with red. I don't know why I'm complaining. I'll be burning them later.

She pushes her hair back from her face and looks at me intently. Like she's waiting for me to say something.

– Stop it.

Her gaze drops. But I can feel she's still waiting for an answer to a question she hasn't asked. She assumes I know what it is. I do. I ignore it. I wipe some of the red from her face.

She holds her hand up and plays with the diamond on her finger. She looks almost worried.

– It's dirty…

– Clean it on the sheets.

She pulls at them and spits on them, cleaning the ring until it's clear and shining again. Leaving another messy red patch on the gold. My body is cooling now. My heart is pounding less and less. I let my eyes close.

*

He's sleeping. I bite my lip. I know he doesn't like to be woken. I'm just a little on edge. He should've told me what to do before he went to sleep. I sit up and look around the room. It's beautiful here. He's so lucky to have a place like this on standby.

I move over to the window and, turning to make sure he's sleeping, move two of the curtains open wider, letting the sunlight stream across the floor.

He lies there naked, breathing peacefully. I want to wipe the blood off his body. Off his face and neck. But I don't want to risk waking him. I look outside.

I don't know if I'm checking to see if there's anyone out there or if I'm checking that everything is still real outside this room.

Outside. It's beautiful. Colour everywhere. Not the plastic, electric mixed-together-in-a-factory colourful that you get in cities. This colour was born vibrant. Untainted by fumes or noise or people. This place exists in a space that most people only know in childhood. Before tax or calories or cancer. It makes me feel peaceful, yet full of battery acid.

I put my hand on the handle of the long window and push it open. The cool air licks my skin. All of it. Drying it. I step outside and close my eyes. The colours sing to me. Green and blue. Earth and water. The slight breeze rustles the leaves in the trees and makes the water lap against the edge of the lake.

The waves look like tiny hands. Clawing at the shore. Trying to climb out. Like it's trapped.

I can feel the colour creeping over my skin. Trying to find an opening. Trying to get in. The colour touches the fresh cut on my ribs.

I open my eyes and go back inside. Slamming the window behind me. Shutting the colour out. The glass wobbles in its large frame. I'm breathing fast and shallow. I look out to the lake, a sight that would make most people gasp, makes me pant. I decide it's best to keep the glass between me and the outside. At least until he's awake.

83

The focus of my eyes shifts. There's a little smudge on the glass. Red. It's on the inside.

*

The sour light of the lamp stains my eyes. My face is turned to the window. It's dark outside. I've slept for a long time. It's dark outside... The curtains are open. Moonlight illuminates the red mess on the cream carpet. It looks black. In this light you could lie to yourself. In this light it could be laundry. Almost.

I sit up. She's sat huddled with her knees up to her chest, still naked, next to the drawers staring at the floor.

– What's wrong?

She doesn't say anything. Half of her is in shadow. The other half is lit up like a spectre by the moonlight. The lamp doesn't reach her.

– I'm talking to you.

She looks up. Her eyes are pleading with me. I should've told her what to do before I fell asleep.

– There's red on the window.

I look to the window. I don't see it at first. The smudge is tiny. A blemish on our view. I stand, about to wipe it off. I pause and turn to her.

– What's wrong with it being on the window? It's all over both of us. It's all over the floor. The sheets...

– I didn't notice properly. I didn't know... I don't think...we can't burn a window.

Her eyes are back on the carpet. She's starting to panic.

– Let's shower.

I walk over to her and pull her up. We walk to the door. Leaving red footprints. She pauses.

– Shouldn't we...we shouldn't...leave?

– It's not going anywhere. It's time to clean up.

I tug at her. She moves willingly across the hall and into the wet-room. I turn the shower on and push her under the water. Her hair flattens to her head and becomes darker. I slip my hands over her hair and down her body. Rubbing the dried red-brown crust that clings to her body. And mine. Until all of her skin is creamy white again. Not a speck of blood in sight. Her muscles begin to relax. Pink water runs off her head and down her back. I follow it with my finger. It runs down into the cleft of her buttocks. I follow it with

84

my finger. She stands with her legs wider. Like she knows I want her to. The water runs down her thighs and calves. I keep my fingers where they are. The water runs off her feet and shows red on the white tiled floor before being sucked down the drain.

*

They come back into the bedroom. There is a smell, like a butcher's shop in the air. The smell of raw meat. They stand naked, looking at the scene before them.

   – We should put the same clothes back on.

She looks at him, obviously worried.

   – But they're…we just got clean.

He smiles at her.

   – And we can clean ourselves again. Come on.

She picks her way carefully around the carpet. Trying to stay on as much of the cream colour left as possible. He walks straight across the big rusty brown patch in the middle of the carpet. He turns to look at her, gingerly picking her dress up off the floor by the little white strap.

   – You need to stop this.

Her eyes dart up to his and she drops the dress.

   – What?

   – You know what. You knew it was going to be like this. You knew what to expect. You were fine with it at first.

   – I know, I just…

   – No. No justs no buts. You're going to stop. Where's that woman who stood before me earlier? You were fierce. You were beautiful. I was proud to be with you. You're going to stop this because I tell you to. You're going to stop this because this is the kind of behaviour that leads to the weak falling. You will not be weak. You will stay strong. Because I say so. Now stop it.

She says nothing. Her face is set and hard. Her eyes start to blaze. She reaches back down and picks up the dress with both hands, feeling its sticky weight. She pulls it over her head and lets it drop down, hanging off her shoulders and breasts. She stares at him and smiles.

   – That's better. Anyone would have thought you weren't grateful for me letting you share this experience.

– I am. I really am. I'm sorry. I feel better now. It's the first time I've ever done anything like this. I'm sorry.

He pulls on his suit trousers and shirt. Hardened in places with the same red-brown crust that stiffened the carpet. His hands are steady as he does the buttons up. One by one.

– It's ok, I understand. I'll always remember the first time I did it. And I didn't have anyone to do it with, mind you! I did it alone. But it's ok because you have me here to help you. Wasn't it fun?

– It was fun. Really fun. I'm fine now. I promise. I would do it again in an instant if you wanted me to.

– I know you would. And we will. He puts his hand on her ribs. Directly on top of the cut. There'll be plenty more of these to come.

His shirt finally buttoned, they look down at the floor. Down at the stained puddle of rusty-brown.

Down at my body.

Naked and ruined for their pleasure.

I look small. Helpless. Cuts over every single inch of skin. Cuts over my arms and legs, young and still with room to grow. Cuts over my chest and stomach, my breasts barely developed. Cuts over my face, undecided over whether it looks more like my mum or my dad.

By now, they'll be looking for me.

He reaches down and picks me up. My whole body draped, limp and hanging, from his arms. She takes the sheets off the bed and bundles them into a ball. She cradles it in her arms like a giant pregnant belly. They take me outside.

If my nose could smell, I would notice the stench of burning. It would remind me of campfires. If my ears could hear, they would pick up the sound of crackling wood. It would sound like winter, inside, everyone together.

With an effortless heave, he dumps my body on top of the flames. If my skin could feel and my throat would work, I'd scream at every lick of flame. Charring me. Cauterising dead wounds.

My body just lies there. Dead eyes open. Not seeing. If only I could. The lake would look alive with the stars dancing in the corpse of the daylight. The trees would be still, welcoming me with open arms to join the unspeaking. And then, them. Tossing their clothes on to the fire, to stand naked in front of me. Holding each other close. Loving each other. Through the flames.

This view would be a great one to have as your last.

Sophie Harris

Hawk Eye

Taking a slow sip from my drink, I scanned the room. A dim light buzzed softly under the shouts and whistles of the bar's inhabitants while the spectacle unfolded. I'd taken a booth near the back of the room and ignored the commotion, knowing it was better not to get involved. However, my 'brothers' didn't have such insight. The men at the bar crawled over each other like ants to catch a glimpse of her. A flash of obscenity before the Hawk Eye system took her away. I gave them all of ten minutes to bask in the brunette's obscene glow before they arrived. The Hawk Eye was quick and efficient; introduced at the start of the reign of the Union, H.E. installed CCTV cameras on streets, work places and even in homes to monitor every possible area of the country at all times. Not a square inch of land was ever left unwatched, which meant that the H.E. always knew what you were doing, when you were doing it and how you did it. It also meant that anyone who happened to be breaking the rules of the Union (and believe me there were many rules) would be severely punished; as the stripping brunette on the counter would find out in approximately seven minutes. Rule 34: Civilians must behave in an appropriate and fitting manner at all times. It was a shame really; she was a pretty young woman with large blue eyes, but that didn't matter at all. Clothed, naked, dying, running, injured, persuasive or unwilling, the H.E. would initiate re-education without a moment's hesitation in the event of a civilian breaking the law.

I turned sharply as a loud crack erupted from the entrance of the bar and sighed; show's over boys. The men at the bar stumbled back in fear and surprise as the door was kicked open and twelve H.E. Officers swarmed into the room. It amused me to see their shock, as if Hawk Eye would really have missed this treat, this excuse to beat civilians to the floor in the name of the 'greater good'. I sat back in my seat, comforted by the idea that the H.E. network had at least proven my innocence; I was free to watch without a moment's anxiety. But that didn't make this feel any more right. As I watched, eight officers held back the men who had been enjoying the little peep show with as much force as they cared to muster; sometimes using chains and knives to emphasise their authority. Two officers grabbed the girl's arms and hauled her from the bar-top to the floor. I saw that pretty mouth of hers connect with the tiling, and flinched. The worst part was to know that I could do nothing. If I objected, I would be re-educated. No-one wanted that fate, and I for one was going to avoid it at all costs. The two remaining officers advanced on the restrained girl as she cried and struggled, their chains raised in a warning to those who planned on being heroes, rescuing the naked princess. The taller of the two officers barked a command in a dialect unknown to the common folk, a language system designed to intimidate the public into submission and to share information without the ruin of surprise. Then, with a shrill whistle, the barbed chains fell upon the victim's back and legs; silver as they fell, they barely kissed her skin before rising for another strike, leaving drops of crimson dew that matched the redness of her cherry lips.

They whipped her with their cruel chains for exactly three minutes, somehow it felt longer. At long last, they released her arms and she stood shakily, indignant; her skin torn and ripped from her education. She looked to them in turn and spat before attempting to run. Rule 74: civilians must show respect to each of their fellows. Another rule broken. The officers grabbed her wrists and threw her back onto the bloodied tiles without another thought. She had not learned enough to be an acceptable member of society; therefore she must undergo more teaching. The military was as brainwashed as the society they served. Most of the men who had been watching the now broken girl strip had left at this point, eager to escape their own re-education while the brunette was beaten; if they were lucky, they would be classed as 'weak in the presence of temptation' and given a mere warning. Of course, the warning in itself was almost as bad. The remaining eight officers stood and watched as though there was nothing wrong with this scene. I sighed and placed my Darby on the table. Another device created by the Union; Darby's were the new non-alcoholic pint of cider. They prevented drunken outbursts and retained orderly behaviour amongst the masses. They tasted as good as they sound. The girl screamed and squirmed under the grasp of the abusive officers as they initiated her second lesson. One knelt over her and pressed the chain to her throat tightly while the second placed at hand on her knee, bending it slightly. This was where I grew weak; no matter how many lessons you witnessed it always had its effect. I watched him re-angle her lower leg and pull sharply, resulting in a dull, wet pop. I fought the urge to retch and placed a hand to my mouth as the young woman screamed in agony. The officers stood back and watched her sobbing on the ground; she was no longer resisting her place as a respectable member of society.

'Thank you, B-Brothers...' she sobbed hysterically, the response as automatic as any anthem is repeated robotically by its country's inhabitants, 'I was wrong. I-I-I am s-sorry!'

Their job was done.

Eight of the officers left, leaving two to clothe the girl and two to analyse the situation. They treated her with care now; not wanting to be seen as villains or cruel justice bringers. They were human as we were and they treated her as any Brother would treat his kind. Rule 74: civilians must show respect to each of their fellows. When she was dressed and led out the two officers left approached me and raised a hand to their brows in sincere salute.

'General Washe, we did not expect to find you here. The Disruption has been re-educated and escorted back to her home. Permission to return to base, General?'

I merely nodded and watched them leave.

Anthony Cerrato

Run

Shit.

Down again.

I scrape my hand as I fall, the gravel covering my bloody palm. I hear the dogs somewhere behind, so I run, as fast as these useless sticks will carry me. One foot in front of the other, left right left right left right until my legs are bloodied stumps left right left right until my lungs collapse and I hit the floor.

Run home, Alex. Run as fast as you can and don't look back. Forget about the dogs. Forget about the cars. Forget about the guys with guns. Forget about what they'll do if they catch you.

They're close now, I pull myself up a ladder and I climb; hand over hand, until I find myself staring out at the city of Cardiff below.

Should be safe up here.

For now.

I heard my father screaming before his shaking hands woke me. His eyes were wide and bloodshot. He pulled me from my bed and threw a set of clothes at me. He dragged me down the stairs where my mother waited at the bottom in her dressing gown, holding my sister's hand. Both looked terrified.

'John,' she pleaded to my father, 'there has to be another way.'

'No,' he said, pushing them outside towards the car, 'it has to be like this.'

As the cold night air hit my face, I met them for the first time. My father was on the ground before I knew what was happening. My sister's screams filled the air for but a second before she was silenced. My mother tried to fight off the attacking men, but the crack of a baton sent her to the floor.

The men moved around my sister, I tried to call out but my face was pushed into the soil. I managed to steal a glimpse. One of them nodded, a large man with a scar running along the side of his face.

A gunshot.

My parents screamed. I saw my father break free of their hold and charge.

Another shot and he was down.

My mother sobbed.

Another gunshot.

Cold hands grasped at my face as a light was shone into my eyes.
'Well,' someone spoke.
'This is the one,' another replied.
'Bag him.'

I hate mornings. It's warm out, but I keep my hat pulled low and the collar of my coat pulled up. I walk to the closest cafe, my pace matched by the business men rushing to work. It's a nice enough place, comfortable red leather seats, clean plastic tables covered with virgin white cloth and it's quiet. I order a glass of water from the girl behind the bar, she smiles at me. She's cute. I take one of the free newspapers to an empty booth at the back of the cafe, furthest from the windows and put my back to the door, watching the room using the mirror hanging in the corner.

I've moved from the headlines to page seventeen, a little picture and two paragraphs of information. Apparently police are set to catch me any day now. Yeah right. The piece ends with the same bullshit. *Advise extreme caution. Consider Mister Warren armed and dangerous! Anyone with information should call-* I close the paper and slam it on the table.

The headaches are getting worse. I can feel it behind my eyes, pressing on my temples. I take a couple of stolen paracetamol from my pocket and chase them with the water. As the waitress passes I order another. She looks at me funny. Probably sick of me ordering the free stuff all week. I should go somewhere new tomorrow. Don't want to draw too much attention to myself.

The bell above the door jingles and two police officers enter. They order two coffees and sit by the window. The one with his back to me takes his hat and coat off and places them on the chair next to him. The other one keeps his on. His face is a tiny reflection in a dirty mirror but I can tell that this guy's a hard ass.

The waitress approaches them and hands them their drinks. She leans in close and whispers something to the hard ass. He nods to his partner who turns to look at my back. Did she recognise me?

I get up and move into the bathroom. As the door closes I move straight for the windows. I push my elbow against it but it won't budge. I'm trapped. No choice, I'll have to go back out there.

I open the door of the bathroom as casually as I can. The waitress smiles at me. The police officers are nowhere to be seen. But their drinks are still there, along with the hat and coat. A trap.

I realise quickly enough to block the first attack, but not the baton strike from behind. My knees hit the ground and my vision blurs.

'Hit him again,' one of them says. I manage to roll away and kick out. My foot hits something soft. A groin? I don't stay long enough to find out. I bolt for the door, throwing the waitress a look she's not likely to forget in a hurry. As I yank the door towards me a shot is fired. When did police start carrying guns? One of them shouts something. I ignore it and keep on. I sprint down Queen Street and make a right into an alley, pushing myself as hard as I can. One of the officers fires another shot. It hits the wall beside me and my face is peppered with hot dust.

I make another turn, vaulting over a line of bins. Footsteps echo behind me and the police call out again. There is another shot followed by pain in my arm. The force of the bullet sends me into a spin and I'm not quick enough to dodge the dumpster. As I turn over to face the police, the hard ass approaches, holstering his sidearm and taking out his baton.

'I'm going to enjoy this,' he says.

'No please,' I beg, 'you don't understand,' the headache is back, boring through my skull.

'Don't worry. I'll make sure to do just enough to keep you out of hospital.'

'No,' I can feel it boiling to the surface, 'you don't want to do this.'

'I really do.'

As he raises his hand I lose control.

When I opened my eyes, they were stood around me, smiling.

'Excellent', one of them said, a doctor, 'you have taken to the treatment wonderfully Mr Warren. How do you feel?'

'Where am I?'

'Never mind that. Are you experiencing any nausea? Aches? Any discomfort at all?'

'I have a headache.'

'That is to be expected at this stage Mr Warren. Tell me, do you remember anything?'

'Wha-? No.'

'Good.'

'Where am I? Where are my family?'

'As I said, don't worry about that now. Your family are safe. They are waiting for you outside. Now just a few more tests.'

A man in uniform entered the room. He had a line of bright pink scar tissue running along the left side of his face. He smiled at me.

'You killed them,' I said.

'Wha-?' the doctor said.

'My family. They're not outside. He killed them,' the headache was getting worse. My neck felt hot and my temples throbbed.

'Doctor,' the scar faced one said, 'I thought you said he'd have no memory of it all?'

'Just a temporary setback Fuller. Nurse, bring me one 100 cc of inhibitor. Calm down, Alex, it will all be alright soon.'

'No,' something behind them crashed to the floor, 'let me go.'

'Pulse is up doctor,' one of the nurses said, 'brain activity spiking.'

'Get me that God damn serum now!'

'LET ME GO!' my shackles shattered and I fell to the ground. One of the guards rushed forward as the doctor made for the exit. I threw out my arm and the guard was across the room. I needed a weapon, and in a second, one was in my hand. As I raised it, a shockwave crashed over me, sending me sliding across the floor. Fuller stood in front of the exit, arms raised.

'Let's see what you're made of,' he said, injecting something into his arm. He threw up his arms again and another wave washed over me. I resisted this time but still fell. Fuller drove his leg into my side, something cracked and I cried out. He kicked again and again, each blow met with the crack of bone. I threw my arms out and my headache flared. Fuller was down, pinned beneath a set of shelves. I was on my feet. How? I didn't know what was happening to me, so I ran. For two years I ran.

It's been a month since I flattened those two police officers with the skip. What was once on page seventeen of the local newspaper search, has returned to a national front page, news and internet manhunt. It's getting harder to move around. The train stations are crawling with police, and checkpoints have been set up on the roads.

My wound has healed and I'm learning to control it. I can move things now. Just pick them up with my mind and move them. It's the strangest thing. So far I've only done small items, food mostly, but every day it gets easier.

A man walks into me, his shoulder slamming into mine hard. I turn to see him smiling at me. Creep. I'm hungry, need something to eat. I check the pockets of my coat. Empty. I hate stealing, but when

93

you're the most wanted man in the city, maybe even the country, you make do. I wander into the market and pick a stall. The old woman inside won't see me, and even if she did, I'd be gone before she could do anything. I wait for her to turn to serve someone and grab a couple of apples and a banana. As I turn away from the stall I see police move to the door of the market. They've found me. Shit.

'Alright,' someone calls. Fuller, 'Warren is here somewhere. Fan out and find him. Its okay, folks, just stay calm. This will be over quickly.'

Something tight wraps around my neck and I feel breath on my face.

'Lieutenant,' the creep who had knocked into me calls, 'I've got him.'

My temples burn and I feel it again. I push out my arms and the man is forced off my back. A shot is fired and a woman screams. The crowd breaks and there are bodies everywhere. Men, women, children, white, black, Asian. All scrambling for the exit. I become lost in the crowd, just another terrified bystander rushing to safety. I pass a man dressed in military garb, looks American. Trust the yanks to be in on this.

The crowd bursts into the road. There is a screech of tires and a car takes out a couple as they cross. As I am forced into the road I see a young girl fall down. A horn sounds as a truck approaches. I push myself through the crowd and move as quickly as I can. I throw myself into her and our bodies roll out of the truck's path. A woman rushes to me and embraces the girl.

'Thank you so much,' she says before looking at me, 'you're that Warren bloke. The one from the TV. Those army guys are after you,' there is a moment of silence, 'get out of here,' I nod in thanks and move on.

'Warren,' someone calls. I turn to see one of the soldiers approaching. I raise my hands and he points his rifle in my face. The scent of the burnt gunpowder burns my nostrils. It reminds me of fireworks as a kid.

He's nervous. I see the beads of sweat run down his face. He's nothing more than a child.

'Don't move,' he says.

'Where you from son?'

'Shut up,' he moves the weapon closer to me.

'What's wrong junior, it past your bed time?'

'What? No. Shut up,' a little closer.

'You ever seen a woman's breasts kid? Of course not, you're probably gay.'

'Shut up,' he puts the barrel to my forehead. In one move I take hold of the barrel, twist the weapon from his hands and drive my fist into his jaw. I feel bone break and the boy cries out. He'll be alright, lucky for him. I take the weapon, eject the magazine and check the ammunition. I've never used a rifle before but I've seen enough movies to know which end to point at the bad guys.

Fuller is taking no chances. The streets are filled with police, military, dogs and jeeps. I turn the corner to find a group of soldiers in front of me. I open fire before they can issue their warning. Seven shots, four down. I aim for their legs, I'm no expert but it's a pretty good shot. I'm not a murderer, not by choice anyway.

The noose tightens and I am bathed in light. A helicopter flies overhead, a voice echoing from a loudspeaker aboard it, but I don't hear what is said. A police van turns the corner and I throw myself into the lobby of a hotel. The woman behind the desk screams at the sight of the gun. I apologise and move for the stairs. I vault them, four a time, for six flights until I breakdown, rasping for breath.

I can hear Fuller and his goons at the bottom so I drag myself to my feet and continue the climb. My calves burn as the lactic acid works its way through the muscles. I grunt though the pain and push myself on. My breath is quick and shallow, my mouth arid and my eyes watering.

I burst through the door onto the roof of the hotel and am hit by cold air. I can feel the headache starting again. The pressure is building on the back of my neck and behind my ears. I begin to hear a ringing before the pain spreads to my temples and above my eyes.

'Alright Alex,' Fuller says as he circles me at a distance, weapon raised.

'Fuller,' I say. I can hear a train at the station close by. 'Why me?'

'You were perfect. You were the first. You belong to the Agency Alex. Those headaches, the doctor can make those go away. Just put the gun down and come with us.'

'And forget the fact that you killed my family, locked me up for three years and chased me for another two. Yeah, think not pal.'

'I don't want to use force.'

'Neither do I,' I strike out, each stretch of the arm a powerful wave of kinetic energy. Six men are down before the first shot is fired. Fuller is fast. Before I can raise my weapon he is on me. He disarms me with a swipe and knocks me back with another. Someone brings their rifle down on the back of my head and I taste blood. I kick out and force the soldier off balance. With a push he's over the edge. I hope he's alright, but he's not. I hear his body hit a car below, followed by screams.

Fuller strikes again, another jab to my ribs. He's strong, stronger than he was last time. My legs buckle and I fall. He brings his foot up and drives it for my face. I managed to roll behind a chimney and catch my breath. Fuller laughs.

'You might not need them,' he takes something from his pocket, 'but drugs have their benefits.'

He injects himself with the needle of blue liquid and stands silent for a moment.

'This is a special blend,' he says, sending a wave of energy over me. His body crashes into me and we tumble like lovers, his weight pressed against me. My breath stops in my chest and my vision turns double. Fuller pulls his arm back and punches, three times, into my face. As he draws his elbow back for a fourth blow I take his wrist in my right hand and snap his arm with a blow from my left. He stumbles backwards and I move away.

'Hold it right there,' he says, sidearm raised, 'don't make this any harder Alex. There's nowhere left to go.'

'There's always down,' I laugh. He fires. The round strikes me in the soft tissue of the shoulder. I stick out my arms and use all my will to throw him from the building. As I fall over the edge I see his body do the same. I take a single breath before my body slams onto the roof of the passing train. I brush myself off and sit down as the train rolls away from Cardiff into the night.

When the news reports this tomorrow, I will be in London.

I will heal. I will train. I will wait. And I will have my revenge.

Stacey Taylor

Viva Las Vegas!

For some, the Barry Manilow concert might have been the last straw, and an acceptable reason to end things, but Linda knew she was going to die before she listened to Mr Manilow crooning for two hours about showgirls and women named Mandy.

She felt like she had to do something touristy before jumping, otherwise what would be the point of going to Vegas? It would have been such a waste and she could easily have jumped in front of a train at home.

She cringed when she thought of the cost of flight tickets. It was so expensive and it wasn't even a direct flight – she had to stop in Denver. Denver had never been on her list of places to see before she died, but she supposed not everyone had been to Denver, so it was something, at least. It always frustrated her that it was cheaper to fly to the East Coast from the UK and not the West, but she'd gone through the trouble of going all the way to the West Coast and she was going to make the most of it. Some people didn't have holidays at all and she knew she had to be grateful. There was a recession on, after all.

The sun was hot for October. She had a brief thought about needing to put suntan lotion on, then she realised it didn't really matter.

She made her way into her chosen hotel. It wasn't the one she was actually staying at, but as with most people visiting Vegas - tourists who excitedly picked out which themed hotels they would see shows and gamble at – Linda had picked out which hotel she'd like to die at.

The icy air conditioning hit her immediately. She walked through the casino – they always put them at the entrance – stopping to use the last of her change. A waitress brought her a drink immediately. She liked that about Vegas. You didn't have to be a serious poker player to experience the generous hotel hospitality.

She listened as the dimes clinked into the machine and watched as it lit up and a message of neon congratulations flashed at the top of it. She hesitated before picking up her winnings and carefully put them into her pocket. She took a sip of her fizzing soda and again experienced a small thrill that it was free. Satisfied, she made her way to the top of the hotel and its impressive observation point.

Looking out at Vegas in the early evening sun, she thought that maybe she should wait until dark so she could experience the glitzy Strip all lit up. It would look so pretty in the dark.

Dave had always been told that finding a coin was lucky – it didn't have to be a penny. As soon as he found the money on the floor he knew Vegas was meant for him – it was a sign more obvious than the sparkly 'Welcome to fabulous Las Vegas Nevada' one he'd passed on the way from the airport. It was almost as if the coins had fallen out of the desert sky, like Elvis was sitting on a glitter-filled cloud up above and had decided to throw him some Vegas luck, rolling down money like dice on a Craps table. He took the money straight to the casino – right at the entrance of his hotel. He watched with joy as on his first attempt the money came crashing out of the machine. A passing waitress smiled at him and handed him a drink. He loved Vegas. He excitedly counted out the money. 'We can go and see any show you want, tonight,' he said, smiling at his wife.

'Barry Manilow?' she asked hopefully. He smiled. He'd fancied The Rat Pack tribute show; but he was so happy he didn't care.

Stepping outside he admired the contrast of dazzling lights against the liquorice sky. There were cop cars outside his hotel and an ambulance. Even their flashing lights gleamed in competition with the spectacular hotels. He felt so full of life. Viva Las Vegas!

Jennifer Lindley

Snow

The night falls and with it comes the snow. The air is spiced with apples and cinnamon. You don't notice at all until the first flake touches your lip and then you laugh that winter is here. Christmas and dreams. You stand in the street unprepared, where is your hat, your gloves and scarf? Stand and stare as the snow falls, exploding like wintery fireworks across the world and forget the past. You ignore the wars of the world, the pain and suffering. There is only snow. It cloaks the world with a drowsy forgetfulness and the dark streets and houses fade into an expanse of marshmallow white.

You find me then, here, and you light up like the frosted icicles that glisten down the streets. Laugh. Dance. Sing. See white trees and a glittering blanket that covers the dark rooftops, hear it softly crunching underfoot when we move together and embrace. Snow angels, snow balls and snow men. We play like we once did, like children still do. We kiss for the first time again and again, under the silvering, mistletoe covered trees. You will remember what once you knew and feel your years turning back. You are 35...21...16...11... 8yrs old. Life is easy and long and there is nothing to be afraid of in the falling winter. This night is yours. The world is new and so are our names.

The flakes freeze and melt. They stick to eyelashes and chill your nose but slide from our faces in heated vapours. Hot hands to touch, cold feet to reheat. You laugh and dance in your new world, twirling with the tumbling flakes and playing in the fresh layers. Which carrot? What to make the smile with? Where is the spare scarf?

You turn to me then and smile. Open your mouth to speak but the words don't come, they don't need to. I hear what you say when tell me you want this to last forever. And so it will, because no one can find you here. The snow guards you, and this spinning world is only what you want it to be. You ask me to stay when you know I will never leave you anyway, yet you are afraid that I might drift away like a snowflake on the wind. You decide that is what I can be, and we are so alike that you will drift away too. What does it matter when no one sees us here anyhow?

When dawn breaks you will take one final look. Watch how gold and silver mingle and meet each other as the new day comes and you will see, you will *know*, that nothing has changed and yet nothing remains as it was. You sigh, you understand. You will look upon a different place to what you once knew and carry on walking until the snow melts into the darkness behind your eyelids.

Andrew Henderson

Phantoms

It's cold. And wet. My feet are frozen, socks soaked through. The rain is relentless, howling winds hurling pellets of ice against my face.

I look up the narrow street, squinting to peer into the shadows at the top. I see a man ambling toward me, just stepping out of the gloaming. He's wearing a dark jacket, just like the one *he* always wears with the white stripe going down either arm. I look down at the floor, huddle deeper into my coat, turn and walk back into the doorway of the pub. Don't want to look too eager. Play it cool.

It's not him, I tell myself. Of course it isn't.

I have half a hope that he'll turn up, with absolutely no reason for him to, yet at the same time I fight with myself to quell such aspirations. They'll only lead to disappointment.

I glance up the alleyway again. Small, hide-away pubs flank its cobbled path.

There's no one there.

Disappointment washes from my scalp to my empty gut. Whoever it was must have gone into one of the other bars. It doesn't matter though, because it obviously wasn't him.

Tonight is not the night to be standing on a street corner handing out flyers. The people that pass are too busy running to get out of the rain to stop for a poxy fucking flyer. I feel my misery etched on my face, and it's no wonder people don't want to stop for me. The thought makes me laugh sardonically. All I can think about is being in a warm bed. Okay, if I'm honest, all I can think about is being in a warm bed with him.

There are a group of people brave enough to test the elements huddled in a knot a few yards away, puffing on cigarettes, and I swear I see his short curls, the copper sheen on his brown hair. This time I do not look away, and the illusion is swiftly broken.

I go inside the pub to warm up and to speak to the barmaid. She makes me coffee to warm my hands, and soon I am heading back out into the cold. As I walk out through the door, I catch a snippet of his accent, and turn to the small group sat near the entrance. You're being stupid, I berate myself. If he had come in you'd have seen him. But still I have to look.

Of course, it isn't him. Not one of the people sounds the slightest bit like him. These phantoms keep haunting me; or rather this phantom keeps haunting me.

The frustration I feel is like an entity in its own right; it is like my dark half, consuming me, feeding from me until it is strong enough to break out. This pondering, this pining; it isn't like me. If I knew, one way or the other, it wouldn't be like this. Does he like me? It seems such a childish thing, even in my own mind, but it is still the case. He seems interested when we are together. But is he just being friendly? He's not here for long, a year at most. He won't be looking for a relationship, and neither am I to be honest, but I'd still like to see him in that capacity. Friends and lovers.

I check my phone for the umpteenth time, stamping my feet to try to get the blood pumping a bit more. Nothing. Not a text or a call, and not just from him, from anyone. Only an hour to go though. That's something.

The windblown rain slices my cheeks as I turn up towards the top of the lane. Why am I here? There's no one around, no point to me standing in the cold for hours on end. Maybe I should just go. But I need the money, at least for now.

Finally someone passes, two lads, but they don't even offer me the courtesy of looking at me. I mutter under my breath about the state of human nature, about what arseholes people are.

I go inside the pub and ask Jo for some more coffee. She tells me to stay inside for a bit, so I do. My phone buzzes in my pocket, and my heart rate increases ever so slightly. Great, my own body betrays me.

Alas, it is just a text from a friend, not the friend I wanted it to be. I reply slowly with half-thawed fingers, shove my phone back in my pocket and make my way outside again.

An hour goes by in pretty much the same way; my senses conspire against me, playing mean tricks with light and shadow, sound and scent. Yes, even in the rain I catch a waft of his heady smell. There is no way to describe it, but clean and fresh. Not soap, not aftershave, just the aroma of his skin.

The rain finally stops, but it doesn't matter, I'm already drenched to the core. The moaning wind is my only companion, keeping other, more sensible people safely inside where it is warm and dry.

My eyes drop to the floor, and misery begins to creep through my consciousness like an uninvited guest. I watch the water run along the gutter, carrying with it dead leaves and cigarette butts. It is almost twelve, the witching hour, and my time to turn into a pumpkin.

He's not coming.

Don't fool yourself; he never was going to come.

I heave a sigh, literally shaking myself out of my sorrow. A cig, I think. I fish in my pocket and take out a fag, light it with shaking fingers, struggling with the flame as it sputters in the wind. I finally get it to light, taking a deep drag and holding it for a while, letting the smoke slowly trickle from my mouth and nose.

Fuck it. I'll see him tomorrow anyway.

My feet drag on the floor as I turn to go in. I hand the remaining flyers to Jo and collect my wages, making small talk before I have to go.

The door opens as I reach for it.

'Sorry,' I mumble, not even glancing up. It's okay now, I don't have to be cheery. I let my dejection take me in its arms.

'Hey.'

A wave of red passes behind my eyes, pounds at my temples and at my neck. It takes my eyes an age to reach the man's face, and when they do my pulse quickens even more. Moss green eyes, lips like a wet dream. My feet suddenly feel as if I have dipped them into the Mediterranean sea; the cold, the tight knot of anxiety tinged with slight despair that sits in my stomach, all of it is gone, stripped under the light of his smile. My pores open, soaking up his heat like a lizard basking on a rock. The wind dies down; Eros has stopped beating his wings for these few precious seconds. Or perhaps it is his wings that brush the inside of my stomach.

I feel a grin stretch across my face and can't seem to help it.

'Hi.'

Sally Thomas

Left Behind

You sit in the shower cubicle. You do not move. You let the hot water fall onto your naked skin and slowly trickle down your body. You catch your reflection in the mirror opposite and stare at the tired old woman that stares back at you. She continues to stare at you until the mirror steams up, and she can no longer see you. You let your head fall onto your chest; the jets slap the back of your neck. For the past six months you have done the same thing every morning, it helps you to accept you are still living. At some point you will get out of the shower and stumble your way through the familiar route into the dirty kitchen. Thursday's dishes will still litter the counter. Your feet that were clean, will now be grey, thanks to the unkempt floor that you tread on. It's Sunday but you don't know that, it doesn't matter to you what day it is, for you they all roll into one. Getting through minutes is all you need to do. Minutes that turn into hours, hours that turn into days that become weeks and eventually months. You do not know what month you are in. Maybe it's December, you enjoy December, you always have. You chose December to get married ten years ago. Your friends all opted for summer weddings, but not you, there was something so much more romantic about the Christmas season. You wanted the fairy-tale wedding, a castle setting that was home to a grand banqueting hall filled with candlelight and not forgetting the roaring fire of course, incessantly burning in the background to add to the ambience.

December was also the last time he was here. Cold and icy December, Christmas trees and holly, the smell of him, that warm comforting citrus smell of his signature aftershave that you used to love so much. You could smell him before he had even taken you in his arms, and when he did eventually scoop you up like a small child it was that smell that made you feel protected, made you feel safe.

You walk to what you believe is still your secret hiding place and you pull out a bottle of vodka. You rely on this precious liquid. Liquid that stops your hands shaking, that allows you to wallow in your own self destruction. You slowly unscrew the bottle and pour out the contents. As you pour you catch another glimpse of yourself, this time in the crystal glass that you have chosen to pour the contents into. Sadly for you it is one of the glasses you choose to bring out for special occasions, so it is shining, shining on the old bitch's face. God, how you detest that haggard face. You thought you had left her in the shower didn't you, but she's right there, she's always there. She's fucking following you. The bitch is following you.

You pick up the glass and use the strength you have left in your body to throw it at the wall opposite. It misses and hits the cooker instead. You begin to laugh hysterically, you laugh until you wet yourself, you laugh until your stomach begins to beg for forgiveness, you keep laughing. Laughing until laughs turn into uncontrollable sobs that rack your body, until you need to vomit. You throw your arms around your waist and grip hold of the pain that sits there slowly and painfully eating your intestines. You wretch and manage to vomit into the kitchen sink, splattering Thursday's dishes as you do. You slide down against the kitchen cupboards sitting in your own urine and your vomit stained clothes. After you have sat for a while you eventually manage to lift yourself off the floor. You take another glass and pour some more of the bottle into it. You throw it into your throat and it hits your intestines hard and fast.

You then stagger towards the lounge with your dirty pyjama bottoms falling from your emaciated waist. You walk towards the stereo that has not been touched since that day in December and press play. You cradle your weak body in your arms and take in the lyrics that reverberate from the speakers. For the tiniest moment they soothe your aching limbs. You look around the familiar lounge and take in the photographs that consume your space; it's always the oval shaped frame that spears your fragility the most. The one of him alone, staring back at you in his full uniform. His handsome face continually pierces your heart. If you stare long enough you will recapture December 2nd. You brought forward Christmas because he was only on leave for a month. He had no choice but to return on December 4th. The army do not give choices.

You momentarily cringe at their advertising campaign. Posters and television adverts that turn your stomach. Posters that tell young boys to make the right choice. You think what the posters should really say is *Make the right choice and end up dead, but die a proud soldier knowing that you did it for your country. Don't fret about your grieving wives who will also die when you do.*

Ten years ago your mother tried to warn you what you would be letting yourself in for when you married a soldier. In light of your choice of the time of year to wed she positively revelled in an opportunity to highlight how Christmas had always been your favourite time of year, that right from childhood through to adulthood your excitement at the festivities had never altered. You remember her asking you the night before your wedding if you were certain of what you were doing? 'Louise, darling when you marry a soldier you take on the government too, for he is already married to them and will need to report to the front line no matter what time of the year it is. Wars do not stop for Christmas'.

That's the funny thing about parents – they raise you for twenty years and yet don't really know that much about you when it comes to falling in love. If your mother had known you that well, she never would have asked the question, she would have known you well enough to know that your love for him was unquestionable. He was your soul mate, your best friend, he knew you inside and out. He made your heart race every time he came near, and after ten years each time he came home on leave, he still had the ability to make you feel like you were falling in love with him all over again.

Your mother does not understand that intensity. Her marriage to your father was purely out of convenience because she had been pregnant with you. You know that she had experienced a special love once. You had heard his name mentioned a few times over the years and you remember the anger in your father's eyes when it was. Your mother had repressed any love she once felt for that man deep down inside of her and had told you many times that love belonged in fairy tales. She said *It was not possible for that sort of love to exist in the real world; too much of real life gets in the way.*

You pick up the photo and sniff the frame in the hope that you can still smell him, but it smells of dead wood. You put your ear next to the frame in the hope that the picture will offer you some kind of reassurance, that this pain will disintegrate and stop haunting your body. You continue to have your ear pressed against the photo as you sway slowly around the room rocking to and fro in time to the music. Your tears begin to fall slowly onto your stained pyjamas as you dance with him. You feel him touch your face and gently brush his fingers across your fringe, down your cheekbone and over your mouth. You melt into his arms until you can smell him. His warm citrusy scent engulfs you and you breathe him in.

The music stops and jolts you from your dream. You are quickly brought back to reality again. You can hear laughter coming from the hallway. Your son has returned from school with a friend. They walk into the lounge and are faced with a scene that no teenager should have to witness. There is a look of sorrow in his eyes but you can not bring yourself to make eye contact with him. He reminds you too much of why you are still here. Voices in your head, telling you that you have to go on for him. He is your number one now. You cannot tell those voices that he is not your number one. You are too ashamed because you know that is what you should feel but you don't. How long is grief supposed to go on for anyway? The so called support network of family and friends make you feel like you have drawn out your grief for far too long. You should be moving on now. Instead your grief has driven you to become an alcoholic mess and the tiniest fraction of the woman you once were.

Each time you want to make eye contact with your son, you cannot bring yourself to do so. You know that the minute that happens you will have to tackle the bitch in the mirror. You hear your son saying goodbye to his friend at the door and you feel a twinge of guilt inside you but you are not ready to be responsible for that guilt so you quickly suppress it. Your kind hearted son comes back into the room and lifts your crumpled body off the floor. He gently props you up holding onto your brittle frame and walks you slowly to the bathroom. Here, he runs a deep warm bath hoping desperately that it will soothe your weary body. He removes your soiled clothes and gently lifts your weakened body into the bath. He then takes a small white flannel and washes your face. He walks away, only leaving you momentarily so that he may clean up Thursday's dishes and mop the dirty floor. He starts by clearing the broken crystal as naturally as somebody washing a mug.

He has an important assignment to complete for his English homework but he won't have the time and will be prevented from sitting his exams because his coursework will have fallen behind. He will celebrate his sixteenth birthday next month but you will not be here to celebrate with him. You will be assigned to a psychiatric hospital the night before. You will blame your son and shout expletives at him when they take you away. Your son will take this hard and fall even further behind on his school work. A year from now, when he cannot get employment due to a failing economy and a lack of qualifications he will make the right choice and enlist in the Army.

Charis Lippett

The Day Liam Took the 39 Bus to Town

Once upon a time Twitter didn't exist, Facebook wasn't around to keep you up to date with your friends' pointless photo albums, and social networking was a thing only forty-something, upper class, housewives did with their debutante daughters. If you wanted to record your spontaneous and irrelevant thoughts for prosperity you had to write them down on paper. And Liam Hadley did just that.

His little, black, leather bound notebook slapped against his thigh with the rest of the contents of his satchel. That's what he called his man-bag, a 'satchel'. Everyone else called it a man-bag, because, really, it was a man-bag; he just hated to admit it. And at any moment, the notebook would be ready to be pulled from the lining of Liam's satchel and thumbed open to the nearest blank page and scrawled upon. What he wrote was never of any consequence per se; he mainly wrote about his intimate observations on life, and: 'Fat women shouldn't wear suspenders' was one such observation.

He sat there under the bus shelter staring at the folds of fat spilling over the top of the lace trim of her stocking. He sputtered and choked as she blew her cigarette smoke out of the corner of her mouth and into his face whilst she traced the bus times with her free fingers. He stared at her faded, plum lipstick smeared into the corners of her mouth, and watched the sun bounce off the grease nesting in the parting of her lank fringe. He'd seen girls in this state before when he waited in line for the campus bus to take him from his halls of residence to his lectures. He never did get well enough acquainted with any them to know why exactly they chose to stay out until 8am, but there you have it.

The 39 bus pulled up and the fat girl stubbed out her fag on the metal frame of the shelter and coughed her way onto the bus, flashing a bus pass at the driver and slumping into the first available seat she could find. Liam followed. Filtering through to the back of the bus, he removed his notepad once again and started writing some nonsense about the number of tired faces on the bus, and reclined his sandy blonde hair against the window for the thirty-five minute ride to the town hall.

'The town hall would look amazing painted blue' was all that he wrote down before stepping off the bus and into the spring sunshine. The sky was a vibrant shade of blue today, like butterfly blue he decided. What butterfly blue looks like exactly to any other man is not certain, but to him, the sky was of such a hue and that was that. And as he walked around the side of the town hall, he found a patch of grass by the fountain and laid his satchel down and reclined down next to it. From where he sat he could see all the pretty builds in Cardiff, that's what his mother called the town center: 'the pretty builds', as if the Capitol Center wasn't pretty, nor the dock, nor the twee houses in Old St. Mellons. But there you have it, he couldn't shake the term from his head, and knowing that this spot was his mother's favorite made him feel somewhat closer to home. He sat facing the town hall, with its big bell standing directly behind it declaring the time. Twenty past twelve, lovely. The sound of the water hitting the fountain trough behind him sounded, to him, like a rapturous applause after a concerto piece he heard performed on the telly, so he wrote that down in his notebook too.

A shadow formed over his scrawl and he looked up abruptly to see the caster. A smile spread wide across his face as her form became apparent in front of the bright sunny glow behind her. Liam was rather fond of Katharine, with her pretty white sundress and green bow in her hair. Kat crossed her flip-flopped feet in front of her and rested her backside on the grass next to Liam. Katharine had a notebook too, but hers was filled with drawings of tall buildings and trees. Her teeth seemed particularly white today as she smiled shyly at Liam, and he thought how nice it would be to be able to keep his teeth as white as hers. He must ask her what toothpaste she used, but not now, now was not the time to talk about toothpaste.

She grabbed a slim, little tin from her hessian shoulder bag and opened it to reveal the many different pencils and charcoal pieces she used to form and shade the images in her notebook. Without saying much at all to each other, they just sat there in the sunshine together, she engrossed in accurately reproducing the figures sculpted on the town hall, him filtering through his lecture notes and jotting down an occasional observation about his surroundings in his little, black, leather-bound friend.

He wasn't expecting what Katharine said next.

'I want to draw you,' she said matter-of-factly with her ginger eyebrows furrowed on her forehead.

'But you don't like drawing people, you think faces are ugly.'

'Yes, but I want to draw yours.' And so she did. Liam wasn't exactly sure what to do. He was very aware of his non-architectural like features and his inability to stay still for more than two minutes at a time. Surely a beautiful column or an intricate branch was far more interesting to draw than his face? Unsure of how to compose himself, he simply continued to swat up on Marxist theory whilst Kat scribbled the outline of his jaw. And that's when she touched his face, his nose to be precise. She had shuffled her body until she was sitting cross-legged in front of him face to face and placed both hands on his jaw as if inspecting it for cracks or blemishes. She ran her index finger from the bridge of his nose down to the tip, tracing its contours and bumps and hmm-ing as she did so. Taking her thumb and index finger, she tipped his chin to the left so as to see his profile. His smile caught her off guard, it caught Liam off guard too if he was honest with himself. He liked her touching his face, and he liked meeting her eyes and seeing them smile right back.

Pink surged up her neck and settled on her cheeks as she promptly gave him back his face and shuffled back into position beside him and continued to scratch away his form and outline on paper. Liam watched as her left hand wrapped itself around the right hand upper corner of her notepad and he noted the colour of her fingernails down in his own: 'Katharine is purple like her fingernails.' Reading it back to himself he knew it didn't make much sense, but that was of no consequence to him, not many of his little notings made sense, but they seemed weighty somehow, almost poetic.

As the sound of 2B pencils scratched against the surface of the paper, and the sun beat down on his face, Liam decided to lie back in the sun. He slapped his books shut and shoved them in his bag, and with more confidence than he usually displayed, he cleared Katharine's lap and rested his head on it. Neither blushed or shied away from the repose, but rather, Katharine placed her notepad on the grass next to Liam's bag and started to swirl circles in his hair with the butt of her pencil.

After a while, the two of them just lay there, both flat on their backs and staring up at the sun. Liam could hear Katharine's heartbeat through her belly and let his head rise and fall with every intake of breath she took. They must have laid there for the whole afternoon because Liam started to feel the chill of the sun setting behind the town hall, and he felt the spring breeze start to nip at his bare ankles. He hadn't written anything in his little notebook for at least three hours. As Katharine drew herself up and started gathering her things, he reclined on his side with his arm propping him up and just watched her. She slipped on her pale pink cardigan and let the sound of tin and plastic clunk together as she drew her hessian bag over her shoulder and got up to leave. Liam thought she was the most beautiful thing he'd ever seen. And she was quite beautiful, really. He wrote this down in his notebook.

Liam stood up to say goodbye, leaving his bag and books on the grass for later collection. He stood with his hands sort of half by his side and half in the air in the space by his ribs. He clenched and unclenched his fists and started to flap his arms in small waves as if he were attempting to take flight. He didn't understand exactly why he was behaving in such a peculiar manner, he'd never mocked a bird before in such a situation, but his hands couldn't seem to stop, and Katharine's smile just unnerved him even more.

And before he knew it, she stepped closer to him so that her face was only centimeters away from his and brushed her lips against his cheek. His arms stopped waving around and fell like dead weights to his side. Her face still lingered closely to his and he could feel the heat radiating from her cheeks. As her nose moved to brush his he placed his flat palm around her rib cage and pulled her in closer so that his lips firmly pressed against hers. With his eyes closed and his kiss on hers he could feel the heat rise from his chest, up through his neck, and into his ears. After about three seconds he let her go and they both smiled and blushed and mutually stared down at her flip-flops.

'Well, bye then,' was all Katharine could muster before she turned and started running as if to catch a bus. She then resumed a steady amble before she got to the end of the green as she turned to wave to Liam. He sat back down on the green, still watching her wait for the lights to change at the pedestrian crossing, and flipped open his notebook to the first blank page he could find.

Rachel Shepherd

Blanket

He looked at his face in the rear view mirror. Two blue eyes stared back. Loosening his tie, he opened the car door and stepped out into the rain, pulling his briefcase out from behind him. The rain dragged his shoulders and neck down so that his body was hunched up and strained, closed together as though he was under an invisible umbrella. He raised a hand to his face and pulled the skin down so that his eyes were forced upwards to look at the sky.

It gets later and later.

It's just the project we're on now. It won't be like this for long.

I don't see you anymore.

That's only because you're stuck in the house all day.

He leant over the back of the sofa and kissed her on the head; letting wisps of blue hair tickle his face. She was curled up, her legs in an L shape covered by the red blanket that they had bought in Spain. The one she always covered the black sofa with to make it look friendlier; if a sofa could look friendlier. She had insisted it did, along with all the other crap she had bought. Teapots, elephant cushions, multicoloured fairy lights; so much clutter. How could objects, small unnecessary objects fill up such a large space?

They waste electricity.

You waste electricity.

That doesn't make sense.

You don't make sense.

She had laughed for ages about that. He had never really understood why.

This time she didn't smile. She did however move herself away, pushing herself more into the corner of the sofa, almost as if she was falling into it. If that happened, would he find her stuffed down the side, like a sock or some loose change?

I mean, once you find a full time job it won't feel like this anymore.

That had been three weeks ago.

The rain continued to hammer down. He stepped over a puddle, careful not to get his new leather shoes wet. Weaving in-between cars he made his way to the door. A woman stood under the overhang to the apartment complex, leaning against the white walls in a black suit, cigarette in one hand, phone in the other. He nodded as he walked past to use his card on the door.

He should have got it, I should have got it, fuck! I mean it's not exactly hard is it? ... Yeah I know, a percentage of that money would have been...

The door shut behind him. He stood there, dazed as he was bathed in light, his eyes blinking. He shivered, shaking the wetness from his clothes, and continued to stare up at the light. Something touched his back and he stumbled forward.

Sorry, wasn't paying attention.

He nodded and moved away from the door, finally raising a hand to call for the elevator. She smiled at him.

One of those days isn't it.

Yeah.

Bloody weather. Think everyone gets like this when it rains.

Probably.

Did everyone? Well, he knew the answer to that. He knew that answer but he hadn't wanted to argue. Who argues about the weather?

He knew the answer to that too.

The doors opened and she stepped inside. Going down, he said, shrugging his shoulders at this other silly mistake. She smiled, pressed a number and the doors shut on her, her face turning to look down at her phone in the last split second. When the next one arrived, he stepped inside and pressed the up button. It always felt so long when he stood in there. When around people, he often took out his phone, just so he wouldn't have to make small talk. He would be standing there with his phone out, composing a message that he wouldn't be able to send because there's no signal in elevators. Once out, he would just delete the message and walk away, smiling politely at reception or to whoever would open the door for him to the car park.

17th floor.

It's not right that people can live so high. I mean, we can live higher than birds. I just don't think that's right.

She was standing at the window, her nose pressed to the glass.

You'll smudge it.

Her face pulled back and her mouth opened. Automatically the glass steamed up and she smiled and began to draw a bird on the glass.

We should cover the whole glass in birds. Look, stand here.

Some of tenants who were passing by had begun to stare and he had given them an apologetic smile.

He stood there now, looking at where she had stood all that time ago; when they had first moved in. A tentative hand pressed against the cold glass and his eyes seemed to look down across the wet city streets. Only one thing was in his mind. The birds weren't here anymore.

He finally reached the flat and pushed on the door, only to meet resistance. He paused, frozen in place. After about a minute he tried to find his key. It was hidden at the bottom of his brief case, along with screwed up pieces of paper and empty crisp packets. He needed to clean it out. He'd do that tonight.

He sat down on one of the black sofas and placed his feet up on the coffee table.

Tomorrow he would go out and buy a red blanket.

Andrew Paul Lambert

O red fruit, ivory, fine timbers

The Song Of Debora

Like most children I had always loved the ocean. There is something alluring about its duality; primal brutality and peaceful tranquillity, destructive yet cathartic. It was a passion that I shared with my mother. We would sit for hours on a tartan picnic blanket, watching my father swim, secretly hoping for the tides to take him away. There was never so much as a subtle undertow. Even so, it is undeniably sublime, and that was one of the reasons that I had been drawn to it. Well, I say that was *one* of the reasons, the main one had been self-preservation, or more aptly, enforced self-preservation. I didn't think that my father cared but obviously he was not keen on the prospect of me being blown to pieces after all. I'm not surprised really. The more I think about it the more I realise that it is typical of his behaviour; he never had respected my wishes. Thankfully, things had turned out quite well, although I had failed to take one thing into account; seagulls. I now realise that I also *hate* seagulls.

That's about the only thing that my father and I have in common. He spent most of his time at the beach shooing them away, shouting one of three comments.

'Filthy scavengers' (sternly kicking sand).

'Nowt but winged rats' (sternly at the ocean).

'Connie, watch the sandwiches!'

He didn't possess the eloquence of William Blake but it's about as close as he ever came to making an intelligent statement. Some are born intellectuals; he was good with his hands. Perhaps that was why my mother was attracted to him, quite ironic really.

I looked out into the blustery spring afternoon. The sea-spray enveloped my nostrils as I pondered life, and seagulls. Waves crashed as the tide drew closer, engulfing the sand below. Walls crumbled and castles fell, retreating into the foam. I couldn't help but wonder what lurked below the surface. How many Nazi bombs had been covered by the tides, laying in wait for an innocent footstep, or a curious prod. The indecisive flapping of the victory bunting drew my attention across the promenade. The war was finally over. I should be happy but somehow I wished it would return; fear and apprehension were far more intoxicating than banality. I felt morally perverse for thinking it, but the truth often is.

The Americans had already begun to depart, taking with them any trace of the exotic. It was the dawn of a new era; time to adapt or stagnate. I was never very good at stagnating but I guess that no one really is. It's just a state of mind that you become accustomed to. I'm not ashamed to say that the war was the best thing that had ever happened to me. I was relishing my new found independence. Nothing depressed me more than the thought of returning home; filthy mill towns, destruction, mundane patriarchal northern men. I suppose that I could at least find some solace in the fact that I was still free, no matter how temporary the situation might be. The American soldiers had a certain aura about them, an unspoken confidence. I found it to be a highly alluring attribute, as did most of the local girls. I didn't like to cheapen myself like many of them though. I have high standards. Luckily, men are consistently predictable. It has to be the red dress again tonight I think.

Once upon a time, in a grand castle, lived a beautiful Queen. Despite her perfect exterior she ruled the land with sternness and authority. The people of her domain lived relatively happy lives of servitude, and although they lacked the luxuries of life, they had what they needed. One day, a great sorcerer appeared and asked the Queen for her hand in marriage, but disgusted by his appearance, she shunned him. In a fit of rage he invoked a curse, proclaiming that a drought would fall upon the land to punish the rebuke of its heartless monarch. And sure enough, the rivers ran dry and the rains ceased.

In desperation the Queen summoned her most loyal knight, Sir Edward.

'Yes my Queen,' he stated boldly.

'As you know, a terrible drought has befallen our land.'

Sir Edward nodded.

'The culprit is a powerful wizard who resides deep within the heart of the ancient wood. He must be hunted down and killed before the evil of his actions take their mortal toll on our people.'

The Queen took an amulet from around her neck and placed it over Sir Edward's head. He glanced down. It was a gold necklace, from which hung a ruby encrusted, egg-shaped locket.

'This belonged to my mother. It will protect you from the sorcerer's dark magic. If it was not for this, he surely would have cursed me.'

The Queen moved closer and fixed his gaze, 'Please keep it safe and your fate will be the same'

Sir Edward's stomach dropped with trepidation, although he endeavoured to exude an aura of gallantry. Dutifully, he raised his head and accepted the task: Facing adversity was one of the expectations of a brave knight. He was also wise enough to realise that you don't mess with the Queen.

Hannah

The evening was busier than usual; the air was thick with tobacco, beer and expensive cologne. There was a strange atmosphere. It seemed to be a mixture of joy and melancholy. It reminded me of spending Christmas with my family, coincidently, so did the rowdy sailors jostling at the bar. I sat at the piano and caressed the keys. The dress obviously hadn't lost its charm as I had gathered quite a congregation. My mother always said that I had been blessed with the ability to work a crowd.

As I played, Abe stared at me from beside the door. I knowingly avoided eye contact, gracing him with the occasional mischievous glance; a simple tool but men aren't the most complex of creatures to decode. I felt as if there was an octopus in my belly but I tried not to let it show. It's always better to keep the upper hand. God he was handsome, like an exotic Clark Gable. He told me that he had been a Jazz musician before he joined the army, New Orleans' premier trumpeter. We would sit in my room for hours, content in each other's arms. The gramophone played ceaselessly. He would whisper French in my ear as Ella Fitzgerald caressed the other. He made me feel like I could do anything, and occasionally I did.

I finished the number with a flourish and thanked the crowd for their applause. My tips jar dinged with appreciation, accompanied as ever by a few drunken proposals; indecent but equally complimentary none the less. My thoughts raced as the evening drew to a close, consumed by anticipation of the night ahead.

Sir Edward had relentlessly hacked and chopped his way through the briers and branches for seven days and nights. He longed to rest but the gloomy forest was cruel and unforgiving; so was his Queen. His flesh had been flayed and his muscles bruised but his resolve remained true. At last, to his surprise and relief, he tumbled out into an opening. Before him stood an enormous stone tower, at the base of which was a single entrance. He cautiously approached the doorway and examined it; it was solid oak and adorned with the most elaborate ivory carvings. As he reached for the handle it opened of its own accord, the creaky hinges beckoning him in.

His tired arms raised his sword once more as he ventured into the dingy portal. To his bemusement a stone ceiling hung just above his head, and at his feet, the floor disappeared into spiral staircase. Sir Edward hesitated for a second, before commencing his decent into the abyss.

The morning sun warmed my back as I knelt with my head poised over the toilet basin, filled with an overwhelming desire to vomit. It wasn't long before this sensation was realised.

'Feel better' a voice said from beside the wash basin.

I cast an eye to the right. Standing with its back to me was a brown demon. It reciprocated my gaze in the mirror as it squeezed a spot on its chin.

'I'm dreaming,' I thought.

'You might be,' it commented, 'Let's think about it, you're conversing with a brown demon whilst vomiting. That does sound quite peculiar.'

'Yeah, I suppose I must be then. I might as well go with it.'

'Why am I here?' it stated knowingly, wiping its hands on the towel.

'I was going to ask,' I said.

It turned around and perched its bottom on the lip of the sink. 'I'm here to help you clarify a few things.'

'But you're a demon,' I retorted, rising from the linoleum.

'I know. We do have a bit of a bad reputation. It's unjustified really considering that everybody has one of their own. Not many people can see us that's all, and I guess that some folks can wish that they didn't'

I thought for a second, 'Okay. That's an interesting point.'

'You see,' it commented whilst picking wax from its ear, '*your* problem is not facing up to problems, and what you sometimes perceive to be problems aren't, in fact, problems at all. That's a problem. Very problematic that.'

I walked toward the sink to wash my face, contemplating this conundrum. The demon hopped up from the sink and walked toward the door, inspecting its finger.

I closed my eyes and splashed cool water on my face, 'I'm not sure that I understand'. There was no reply. I dried my face and looked toward the door. The spot where the demon had stood was empty, and all that remained was a single pomegranate wobbling on its base. I stared at it perplexed. How did it know that I really craved a pomegranate?

Jephthah

I didn't know what that feeling I experienced was; loss, regret, betrayal, embarrassment? But I decided that I would never put myself in a situation where I could feel that terrible again. Thinking with your heart is a sure way to get it broken. I should have listened to my mother.

'I'm sorry Connie, I really am. It was never my intention…'

'I know exactly what your intention was, Abe,' I interjected, 'that's the worst part.' I should have known better. I tried not to show how devastated I was, or how much he had hurt me but I felt like something had changed inside. It took all of the strength that I had to fight back the tears, but I had to retain my dignity. It was all that I had left and I wouldn't give him the satisfaction of thinking that I needed *him*. I had never felt more like Jane Eyre, though this relationship would not reach a contrived conclusion. That was the one thing that I found less than aspirational about Bronte's novel, how could Jane forgive a man that had intentionally betrayed two women? Every time I read it I was filled with anger at its resolution. Reader, I had no intention of marrying him. My mother always told me to avoid making decisions led by any organ other than my brain. I thought that I had understood what she meant but now I know.

Abe reached for my hand but I shrugged it away. As the breeze caressed my face I stared at the receding waves and imagined that I was somewhere else.

He told me that he was married, and that he and his wife had... I didn't want to hear it. I had no interest in his life. In a few weeks he would be back in America, the conquering hero returning from battle, though I'm sure that the nature of some of his conquests would remain undisclosed. There was nothing here to comfort me, just the remnants of our sordid affair. He spoke for what seemed like hours but I focused on the sound of the lapping waves. Finally, he took the hint and left. I hardly noticed.

I clutched onto a pebble that sat under my palm, rubbing it with a force that could strip the skin from my fingers. I picked it up with the intention of throwing it as far into the ocean as I could but for some reason I glanced down and opened my hand, revealing a brown stone. There was something beautiful about it. I gritted my teeth and dropped it into my handbag. I have no idea why; it just *seemed* right.

The battle had raged in the catacombs of the sorcerer's lair for hours. Sir Edward fought with all of his heart but his opponent predicted his every move.

'There is no use in resisting,' the sorcerer proclaimed mockingly, 'all I wish for is the Queen's amulet.'

'Never,' Sir Edward unconvincingly declared.

'Edward, you really are a fool. Your Queen has sent you here to deliver it to me. The people are dying and only I can end the drought. I am too powerful for you to vanquish. She knows that, as do you. What does your heart tell you?'

Sir Edward mustered his last ounce of strength and drove his sword deep into the mossy bark of a great oak tree. His vision blurred as the world began to spin. Great spirals of red and brown swirled before his eyes like a kaleidoscope, beckoning him in. He fell to his knees with delirium and was filled with an overwhelming longing for his Queen's soft embrace.

Matthew Herman

The Man Who Wasn't There

People are looking. Do I care? I emerge from the cubicle straightening the creases in my dress. My hands smooth the imperfections like an iron as the first rush hits me, and I take a step out towards the room. My world just got bigger; sweet euphoria taking me away, as I simply breathe, feeling alive. The steps I take between the doorway and the sink suddenly become the most interesting part of my day. The grime and mould on the walls are no longer ugly and ignored, but beautiful. A coming together of colours, a meeting of minds, a tribute to what comes. A girl brushes past me, catching my eye in the mirror and giving me a hard look. See, I look different to most people, they don't see the world the way I do. This girl has no beauty in her; long, blonde hair straightened, perfectly manicured nails, fake tan, short skirt, everything about this girl was hiding. She is so perfect she becomes invisible. I'd offer her a line, might loosen her up, be less scared of what people think, but in all odds she'd probably just call the bouncers and that would be my night. I hit the silver circle on top of the tap, relishing the noise and sight of the water as it gushes down, little drops shooting out at a wonderfully random angle from a loose connection. It's the imperfections that make the beauty, that tell the story. It's all in the details. Pay attention.

Washing my hands, and taking delight in the feeling, I check my face for obvious signs. I leave the bathroom floating.

The bar is busy, and people are dancing now, Jesus, how long was I in there? I walk over to the back door, under the vague idea of going outside for a cigarette.

'Ya'alright there love? Lookin' pretty spaced out.'

I freeze like prey, then relax; just some lad being friendly. He's ok, actually quite good looking, in a geeky sorta way. I begin to warm to him and the drugs warm to me, and I can tell he's checking me out. Most guys who aren't into 'typical girls', like my friend from the toilet, are interested. I laugh, relaxed, and because I think he said something funny. He invites me back to his table, sure I'd love to thanks. I fall into step behind him, babbling away, just being friendly and about five faces turn to mine as we get to his table. Never one

121

for awkward talk, I jump down next to one of them and start babbling introductions. They are smiling, I am Christina.

The two girls are pretty enough, and have something to say, which is a rarity. One is obviously the partner to the kinda surfer guy on my right. The guy I met first and the other one are... My train of thought stops. Everything stops. The noise of the bar doesn't die down slowly like in the movies, someone just hits the mute button. In the silence my ears ring, that high pitched whine that you can never place.

The last guy is sitting quite still.

His eyes seem white under my high. I think his hair is short, maybe a crook in his nose, I only have eyes for his. Straight back, he seems to lean forward over his beer, eyes locked on mine, and he keeps leaning, so slowly, out over the table where his drink sits innocent like him. Time stops. He's going to fall off the chair, crumple in a mess at my feet. I can't talk or think, I vaguely register that the guy I met is introducing me, and this one keeps leaning. My mouth is dry. His face is right in front of me, nose almost touching, his nostrils flaring as if he's trying to suck something out of me. I get a smell off him that I can't place, sickly sweet, like chemicals, bitter almost, like the smell in a dentist's waiting room. I blink and he is back across the table, nodding at me in a friendly way as he gets his introduction. No one else can see it, it's for me. He wants me.

My friend is still talking, telling me names now with gentle hand gestures around the table, but adrenaline pumps through me, and my heart is slamming against its cage. Like a bad dream, I'm stuck to the chair. He looks mildly amused by my so recent silence, I think I'm shaking. The others fall back into natural conversation as the drugs turn on me, just ride it out, you're being paranoid. I have to get out of here. He is still watching me, staring, and now he's in my head. Wandering the passages of my intimacy with a delicate giggle, seeing my life at its worst. All the sticky fumblings in the back seat of cars, a thousand images flash through my terror in a second, and he sees it all. He brings it to the surface with ruthless efficiency, exploring my most intimate secrets, laughing at me. Giggling. The introduction comes to him and he stands, leaning over the table, one hand on the back of a chair for support, the other extended towards me in a mock friendly gesture. He sees me. He wants me.

Like someone else is moving it, my hand moves towards his. No

122

one else seems the slightest bit perturbed by this creature, and against all of my instincts and power, I take his hand. It's dead cold, like holding a piece of meat from the fridge, except through that chunk of meat I feel a single beat of his pulse, then the silence again as he smiles.

'Nice to meet you Christina, my name's John.'

Katy Lewis

Stationed

Victoria climbs the station steps to the platform. She stands waiting, the cool morning breeze fighting its way through her dishevelled hair. The clock strikes fifteen minutes past eight. Announcements sound but still she cannot grasp their meaning. Many Spanish suits glide past her on the busy platform, and between them the usual grey faces appear. She sees them every day; same train, same time. They never speak but acknowledge one another. Standing in torn, blood-soaked clothing, they go unnoticed by the crowds.

Victoria locates those familiar to her one by one. The old couple stand hand in hand, a perfect three inches beyond the platform edge with heads held high. Shrouded in shards of glass they clutch each other tightly. She cannot see their faces. Victoria remembers home; how she misses it. She longs for the warmth and touch of the one she loves, never to be seen again.

A little girl circles her feet, as she always does. Her pigtails wrap around her pallid face as she looks up and smiles. She sings what sounds like a Spanish nursery rhyme, but she can't be sure. The language remains alien, although she's resided there so long.

The girl stops skipping around at the sound of her mother's voice. Right on time, mumbles Victoria as she turns left to see a partially naked lady, blackened from head to toe. Now drained of her emotions no tears are shed. Matted hair does little to hide the lady's features, which are clearly disjointed in many places. Eyes cannot be seen through the swollen, red wounds. Little skin remains.

The child runs to her mother, hugging the fragile figure she calls 'Mama'. From behind that pretty girl can now be seen in her true colours; black and red. She shares with her mother the wounds no one could survive. Burns and scalds run down her back. A six-inch section of glass poking from her waist glistens in the sunshine.

The mother grips her daughter looking ahead to Victoria. They stare longingly at one another as life carries on around them. The clock strikes eight. The platform continues to fill with people proceeding with their daily lives. Victoria envies their freedom.

Next to arrive is the young businessman, minus his briefcase. He stands a few feet to the right of Victoria. Hands cupped together, he

124

turns his wedding ring around on his finger. That finger remains the only one intact on his battered, discoloured hands. A gaping hole splits much of his thigh, blood flowing no more. His gaze drifts to the old couple standing tall on the edge of the platform. The speed at which he turns the ring quickens, and his sunken grey face hardens. He doesn't cry. Victoria looks at the gold band, only wishing she could have made it that far.

Twenty-seven minutes past eight, and the train approaches. Slowing in its tracks it creeps along before finally coming to a complete standstill. It casts a shadow over its awaiting travellers, and as the doors open time accelerates. The once-stationed passengers rush towards the entrance, all hoping to be seated for a more comfortable journey. Only the grey-faced minority take their time. Even the old couple first in line step back.

As the last few passengers prepare to step aboard, Victoria looks to her left and sees as many as fifty sullen souls looking from one face to the other, searching for another solution. To the right a few more hover, not wishing to proceed.

The old couple are the first to board, gripping each other's hands tightly. Everyone else follows, heads hanging low. Taking a deep breath, Victoria is one of the last. The atmosphere changes as her left foot touches the first step. A chill cuts through a carriage now filled only with charred occupants. Victoria takes her usual seat, the one next to the rotund boy with a glass-splintered face. After passing the old couple in the front row, the young businessman reluctantly sits to her left. The little girl pops up over the headrest in front, deadened eyes focused on Victoria. She isn't smiling now.

The train begins to move in silence. All passengers face forward, apart from the little girl in locked gaze with Victoria. The clock at the front of the carriage says 8:29. Still there is silence. Counting down the seconds in her head, Victoria starts at 10.

9, 8, 7, 6, 5, 4, 3, 2, 1 …

The sound is deafening. Scraping metal and screeching voices ring loudly in her head. The carriage immediately warms as a red and yellow cloud devours its surroundings. As it closes in she thinks of home. The little girl disappears before her, as does everything else.

Then there is nothing, not a sound.

*

Victoria climbs the station steps onto the platform…

Tamara Winkler

Sea as Blue as Sapphire

I always dreamt of walking by the cool blue sea with the sun bouncing its rays gently against my face and the breeze swishing through my hair. I would walk the length of the beach in my bare feet feeling the sand soften and squish between my toes. I would dream of some distant lover and feel his caress against my skin and think of how things might have been.

Sad though it is, I have never had the opportunity to walk by the sea on my own. I'm a single parent with two children whom I love dearly, but oh how things could have been.

I wasn't cut out for parenthood, it came upon me as a complete surprise. No maternal instincts had I and no understanding of the enormity of what having children would mean. I was young and carefree living life to the full and I fell in love. My husband-to-be was a postman. He loved his job, all that fresh air and nobody telling him what to do. As long as he delivered his post on time nobody bothered him.

We met at a friend's party. I had had too much to drink and was slurring my words. I asked my friend 'Whoooozzatt?' Pointing at Jim with a wobbly finger. Next thing I new I woke up lying next to Jim with a stinking hangover and looking like I had just come back as a vampire.

We got hitched at the local registry office and I was pregnant within a month. By the time I was twenty I had two children, no career and lived in a council flat on a very dodgy estate. Jim would bring home his pay packet, which would just about cover our needs, we would splash out Friday nights with pizza and a video and that was my life.

I didn't mind, I loved my kids, they were fun. We played in the park, made silly pictures at home and dressed up acting out cartoons on the telly. But one day I bumped into an old school chum, Sara. She looked gorgeous. We chatted for a while and I gave her my number in case she was passing and wanted to pop in.

I couldn't get Sara out of my head. How come she looked so beautiful? I took a long hard look at myself in the mirror and didn't like what I saw. I had turned into my mother and I was only twenty-two. I had a haggard look, my hair was lank and my skin pale and lifeless.

I decided from that day on that life would be different. I still made Jim's tea when he came in from work and played with the kids until they were tired but I made time for me. I bought better quality shampoo, put on a little rouge and wore clothes other than jeans at least one day a week. It's not much I know but I had to start somewhere.

I didn't have a job, I didn't have a hobby and I wasn't secretly talented at anything but I was making more of myself day by day.

The next time I met Sara I didn't think she looked so pretty. She praised me on how well I looked and I felt a million dollars. Little by little my life was becoming my own and something I enjoyed to the full.

One day I came home with the shopping and found a note put through the letterbox. Jim had been suspended and was facing prison. Apparently he had been stealing from the post office and had been caught red handed. The money Jim had been bringing home was more than he legally earned, Jim had been stealing post, opening it and taking whatever money was in it or pawning gifts to bring home extra cash.

I never knew of course, Jim always told me that the money was earned in overtime and that I was not to worry. We were never rich you see, so I never did worry. Not until Jim was found guilty and had to face a three-month prison sentence. Jim lost his job and we had to move to another town as his name had been splashed across the pages of the local rag. Other school children began to beat up Jack and Dean. The taunting became so regular that Jack and Dean tried to find excuses not to go to school. That's when I made my decision to leave Leicester and move to Plymouth.

So here I am walking by the sea, bent double by the force of the wind, with my wellies on, crunching the stones under foot and shouting till I am hoarse for Dean and Jack to 'be careful.'

I don't have any more money. I live on the dole, take my children to school, cook their tea, tidy the house and get to go to Kwik Save for my shopping.

There's no point in looking for a job because by the time I pay for the after school care and the rent, bills and food I would be no better off than being on the dole. I content myself with daydreaming, dreaming of walking by the blue sea with the sand under my feet.

Jim got out of prison after serving his full three months. We met up and tried to patch things up but he was a changed man and I couldn't trust him anymore. I tried, for the kids' sake. I wanted them to have their father and to have fun with him. But every time I gave him money for the kids to go out for the day he would always spend it on booze. He wasn't an alcoholic, just changed. Jim didn't think what he had done was wrong, not wrong enough to deserve prison. Jim never talked about prison but I know he had nightmares about it. Jim didn't sleep well anymore and the less he slept the more he drank.

Jim had wanted to be an artist. He had talent and an eye for colour. He had wanted to go to art college but his mother had insisted he go into the army to be a real man. After one stint in Northern Ireland where four of his mates had been blown up by a car bomb he was let out on medical grounds. Medical meaning he couldn't hear an exhaust backfire without hitting the deck and shouting 'get down.' That's why working as a postie was so great. He could get up at the crack of dawn, deliver his post and be back home midday to spend the rest of the afternoon painting, drawing or just dooddling.

I have two portraits of Dean and Jack sketched by Jim. He caught their cheekiness and their sweetness all in one. I can see his resemblance in them, their strength of character and their wicked humour.

It all came good in the end though. Jim came home the moment I wrote to him to tell him I had cancer. He looked after the boys, took over the housework and took care of me. I learned to love Jim in a new way. Just when I had come to the realisation that Jim really was all the world to me, as well as the kids, I was going to have to leave them.

My cancer was non operable you see, caught too late because I didn't have smear tests, I had always meant to go, kept putting it off, making excuses and then when I began to bleed day after day, month after month with no let up I knew something was wrong. I just put it down to poor diet. I took more exercise, got good sea air, became vegetarian, but still I bled. Eventually I decided to see my GP who thought it might be hormonal, some women do go through the menopause early, but just to be on the safe side he would send me to a specialist.

The next appointment for the specialist was three months away. It wouldn't have made any difference as it was too late then anyway the consultant said. I went to that appointment then I had tests done and an X-ray. I saw the consultant about a week after that to get my results. I couldn't really take it in. I had left Dean and Jack in the waiting area playing with the Lego. The consultant was looking at me repeating it again and again. Mrs Williams I am sorry but your tests have come back positive. You have cervical cancer. We recommend chemotherapy and surgery however the cancer is virulent and we may not have caught it in time. He paused. 'Is there anyone with you? Anyone I can call for you?' All I could manage was 'no' and 'thank you'.

I went through the chemotherapy, I had a colostomy bag, I got thin and weak. My left leg began to turn in and my hips began to hurt. I couldn't eat much it made me sick. I tried everything including drinking Guinness but nothing stayed down. After a while I asked for the treatment to stop. I had had enough.

Then came the time I had to plan for my funeral. I knew I was getting bad. I would doze in and out of consciousness, the morphine getting heavier and heavier. I ate little, was bed ridden, I couldn't even go to the toilet; I had to have bed pans. It reached a point that I really didn't want my children to see my like this and decided there and then to say good-bye. I just decided to shut my body down and say good-bye. I have always known human beings can switch their switch, if they want to, if you want to die you really can; you just have to put your mind to it.

I asked Jim to contact Sara. I didn't know why I just knew I wanted to see her before I died. Sara came, she held my hand, she massaged my legs and put peppermint lotion on my feet. I couldn't feel my legs but it just felt nice to have that fresh smell and to be pampered a little.

Sara didn't cry, she just looked at me with her beautiful blue eyes and held me when I needed it. We talked about all sorts of things. I told her about meeting up with her when Dean and Jack were still small and how haggard I had felt when I looked at her because she looked so beautiful. Sara laughed and said, 'If only you had known, beauty is only skin deep. I was really very unhappy when you met me. I had no husband, no children; all I did was work. I was envious of you. I thought how nice it would be to come home to a husband and a family to be with, but I went home to a tidy flat with my TV dinner and a soap on the telly. What I would have given to have your life.'

Sara brought me a deep blue dress and played me mystical music. I told Jim and Sara that it was nearly time. I gave both the boys a kiss and told them to be good children for their dad. And I lay down, closed my eyes and dreamt of walking by the cool blue sea with the sun bouncing its rays gently against my face and the breeze swishing through my hair. I would walk the length of the beach in my bare feet feeling the sand soften and squish between my toes. I would dream of some distant lover and feel his caress against my skin and think of how things might have been.

Ellen Duncan

Witness

26th May 2013

The man looks angry. Even in the dim light from the other side of the coffee shop, I see his lips pressed tight together, the rhythmic flexing of his fingers and the tension in his shoulders rucking the collar of his shirt. I gulp down another mouthful of coffee, bitter and black and just a little too weak, like it always is from Starbucks.

I keep watching. He flips his phone out, squinting at the screen and then snapping it closed again, dropping it to the table with a clatter. I look away briefly, then back to him. He looks like he's waiting for someone. Who? Maybe that's why he's so angry though, so tightly, precariously controlled. I trace the tabletop with restless fingers, twitch at the sound of the door swinging shut.

I turn at the same time the man does, looking to see who has come in. A woman, tall, well dressed and striking, though not pretty; two men behind her. Her eyes flick to the man, the barest of acknowledgements, and she heads to the counter, orders something fancy and noisy. The two men settle silently at a nearby table, the harsh lines and black-and-white of their suits imposing on the warmth of the shop, the smooth curves of the tables and seats. The man is watching her, face intense and arms crossed tight over his chest. The thought of work edges its way into my mind, but my eyes are fixed on his, ears straining uselessly to hear anything he might say, even my shoulders tipping slowly towards him.

She joins him, sitting opposite, tense but not in the same way as him. She isn't angry, but she's not as aloof as she wants to be, either. Something *matters*. They sit like that, facing each other, silent, for several long seconds, and I realise with a jolt that I'm literally holding my breath waiting to see what happens. I force myself to inhale, to take a sip of coffee, to settle back in my chair and relax. Even doing that, I never take my eyes off them.

Finally, he speaks. A name maybe, a greeting. She nods back, flashes a sharp, close-mouthed smile, says something that makes his eyebrows, dark and a little heavy, draw together. I think he asks, 'What do you want?' leaning forward so his arms brush the table.

She pulls something from her bag, papers filled with neat black print, and my eyes ache from the strain of trying to see, though I know I'll never be able to read it. Divorce papers? Maybe, but it seems a strange place to be dealing with something like that, on the edge of a semi-crowded cafe, with two suited men sitting nearby. They look official though, and it fits with his anger, the tension that only exists in unhappy people who know each other too well.

The expression on his face when he looks at the documents – whatever they are – is strange. Angry and resigned and maybe a little afraid, which seems odd, and it twists his face into something uncomfortable. He says something else, a long string of rapid-fire words, and from the way his arms twitch and fingers clench, he looks like he's holding back wide, expansive gestures. She just keeps watching him, and I wonder how they know each other. Maybe they *are* divorce papers, but why the men, who I *know* are involved, and the tension doesn't seem sexual. Bitter yes, and laden with familiarity, but nothing to do with attraction, whether still in existence or long faded. I frown, fascinated, and for all that the tension is bleeding into me, putting me on edge, I stay where I am, intrusive and worried and completely unable to help myself. I'll never find out what's happening, but at the same time I need to watch it play out.

She taps the stack – a centimetre thick – with long-nailed fingers, and leans towards him, intensity finally encroaching on the cool blankness of her face. They stay like that for a long moment, just inches between them, struggling silently, until finally he tips back again, looking tired and resigned, anger reduced to a dull simmer. He shifts, unhappy and uncomfortable and something breaks; he snatches the pen, knuckles white around it, and scribbles his signature in short, jerky movements, pressing hard enough that I almost imagine I can hear the scratch of it over the hiss and rattle of the coffee machine.

He stands abruptly, without a word, nodding to her, his jaw clenched, before turning and leaving. I watch him leave, watch the door click shut behind him before returning my attention to the woman. She looks grimly satisfied, like she has won something after a long time, or maybe won it without being sure that she really wants to. She nods to herself, just once, and digs out her phone. The call is short, to the point, and she leaves almost as soon as she's finished, the suited men following her out. It's a struggle to stop myself entertaining ideas of spies and secret deals, of some strange covert

132

operation, and I gulp down the cold remainders of my coffee, making my own way out, taking the long route back to the office.

19th June 2013

It is a Sunday, some weeks later, when I stumble out of bed and dress in a sloppy pair of jeans and a t-shirt that's one thread away from falling apart. It's comfortable though, and I've been living with Johnny long enough by now that I don't worry about looking good on a Sunday morning. He's already in the kitchen, waiting for the coffee to brew, smiling at me and darting in for a quick kiss before handing over a plate of toast.

'Morning, Kate. I was going to bring it up to you,' he says as I mumble my thanks and slump over the table, muzzy with sleep.

It isn't until I'm nearly half-way through the coffee that I wake up enough to hold a proper conversation, and Johnny knows me well enough to wait until then before handing me the paper, just another part of the weekend ritual. Even with the extra caffeine in my bloodstream there is about a minute where I frown at the front page, not really registering it but aware that I should, that it is somehow familiar, significant. My gaze flicks away from the picture I'm not really looking at and up to the headline: 'Horizon Announces New Power Source'. My eyebrows rise and something in my chest twitches, curiosity and uncertainty of what to make of it. I glance back down to the image, frowning again at the sudden jolt of recognition-disbelief-excitement.

'It's the man!' I yelp. 'The man from Starbucks!' I tap the printed face and wave the paper at Johnny, his bemused expression clearing.

'The angry guy you were talking about the other week?'

'Yeah, that's him!' I shake my head, squinting at the photo.

'Seriously, how weird is that?'

'What's it say, anyway?'

'Last night Horizon Nuclear Power, the UK's leading company in nuclear energy and development, announced that it has made a major breakthrough in the future of power production. Leading physicist John Neil, who has spent the past five years as a researcher for Horizon, made the initial discovery, and he has been working with other scientists throughout the process.

'This development is one of the greatest since the birth of nuclear power,' says Horizon CEO Paul McGowan. 'It's cleaner, easier to dispose of and much more efficient in terms of the input-to-output ratio.'

If these claims are true, the future of energy production could be heading in a vastly different direction.

'It could change the world."

I look up, eyes wide. 'Wow.'

7th September 2021

I really wish he hadn't signed it. Doctor John Neil. There was a reason he was so angry that day in Starbucks. It took me a few months at the time, a few months of following the story obsessively, but I realised eventually that he had signed away all rights to the discovery to the company he worked for. I don't know why he did it, when he obviously hadn't wanted to. Maybe they were holding something over him, maybe there was something else; I'll never know, but it gave them more or less complete control over the project, and government intervention did very little to change that.

What, exactly, did we expect would happen? One company owns the greatest power source in the world. It took a while of course, they were careful about it, slow, but very soon they had governments eating out of the palms of their hands, all across the world.

I'm back in Starbucks again. I still come here a lot. Comforting, I suppose. Johnny comes with me sometimes, occasionally a friend. Changed jobs three times and now I'm working as the manager in a temping agency. It took a long time to find something that didn't have links to Horizon. I'm not radical, I've never done anything, but I don't like them, don't like what they've done to the world. Nothing overt, but it's enough that they can hold it over us like that, that no one can really speak out against them. People have lost jobs, and more.

I flick open the paper left at my table, crumpled and a bit grubby, skim the headlines. Regulations against other power sources becoming more stringent. New power plant being built.

Divisions within the Labour Party – again. Johnny Depp a grandfather now. I click my tongue, rub at ink blurred fingers, glance briefly around the cafe. I don't linger. I don't look closer at the arguing couple or wonder what the woman in the corner is doing on her laptop.

Barry Hogan

A Return to Brighton

I sip my coffee and look at my birthday cards, neatly placed on the windowsill. A breeze comes in through the French doors and the sound of a wind chime can be heard, tinkling delicately in the distance. Yvonne is reading *The Guardian* and a small wrinkle appears between her eyebrows, as it does when she is concentrating. A few strands of hair fall into her face and she brushes them away.

She holds up a cartoon drawing of a millennium bug and smiles.

'Hey, look at this.'

I try to smile.

'It's almost quarter past. Are you going in later today?'

'Erm. Yeah. First meeting is half ten, so no rush.'

'Right, okay. What time do you reckon you'll be home?'

'Erm. About half sixish.'

'Okay. Oh, I think Sue and Tom might pop in for a drink later.'

'Right, okay. That'll be nice.'

I drink the last of my coffee, stand up and straighten my tie.

'Martin, are you okay?'

'Yeah, just a bit tired I think.'

'You sure? Is it your birthday?'

'No, I'm fine. It's just a number isn't it?'

'Lie. That's what I've started doing. I tell my kids at school I'm 21. And they believe me.'

This time I manage to smile back.

I lean over to Yvonne, kiss her on the cheek, and reach for my briefcase. Today it contains a pair of jeans and a t-shirt instead of a lap top and company reports.

Today will be an adventure.

I enter the station, walk over to the ticket machine, and select a return to Brighton. I am about to put my bank card into the machine. Then stop. Better to pay with cash. I board the train, looking around in case there's anyone I know. Not too late to turn back. I could get off at the next stop if I wanted. Maybe go to work. Today could be like yesterday, or the day before.

I enter the toilet and change my clothes. Look at myself in the mirror. Is this t-shirt too young for me? My hair is now more grey than blond, there are a few wrinkles on my forehead, but I keep myself in shape. I look okay. Forty isn't old. But closer inspection reveals dark circles beginning to appear underneath my eyes. I don't feel young though.

I step off the train and onto the platform. The lighting is poor and crisp packets, chewing gum, and cigarette ends are scattered on the floor. It feels unfamiliar. I walk along the street then stop to look around. Weathered Victorian houses that have been turned into takeaways, cafes and newsagents. Some of them have had a fresh coat of paint and the rickety old windows of my favourite pub have been replaced with new double-glazed ones.

A seagull squawks and the smell of fish and chips lingers in the air. I put my hand up to my face to block out the sun and look out onto the sea. The old fishing boats are still there. I remember a conversation beside those boats and feel my lungs releasing a low, troubled sigh. My body slouches and my eyes look down at the floor.

I reach a pub I used to go to.

The wallpaper is peeling at the corners, the carpet is threadbare, and there is a strong smell of damp and stale ale. But when I look at the open fireplace I recall a memory. A forbidden kiss.

I buy myself a drink, take a seat by the window, and open a packet of cigarettes. There aren't many people here. I glance over at the bar. Look away. Look back. We make eye contact. We hold eye contact. I take a drag from my cigarette, inhaling deeply. Here it is, right in front of me, my reason for coming here. I can do this. Smile. The stranger smiles back. Get up. Go over to the bar.

I hurry across the road and look out onto the seafront, and notice a couple walking past. They are painfully thin and are arguing. Brighton.

I look back at the fishing boats. My vision becomes blurred and drops trickle down my cheeks.

We are sitting on the beach, drinking Lambrusco. One of the beach bars is playing a song by Joy Division, our favourite band at the time. It is almost dark but we are still wearing our mortarboards. Yvonne has just dyed her hair blue and had half of her head shaved and I'm wearing tartan trousers and Doctor Martin boots.

Stupidly, we decide to go into the water but don't make it much past our ankles before the waves knock us back onto the shore. We fall over. For a moment I worry that she might have hurt herself, then I realise that she is laughing. We lay on the beach, looking at the night sky. The waves thrash and there are sounds of soft laughter from our friends in the distance. We are both soaked but it is the beginning of a hot summer so we don't feel the cold. I look over at Yvonne and the lights from the pier are reflecting on her face. She is happy.

Ding-ding! Ding-ding!

I realise I am standing in the bike lane and quickly move out of the way.

'Hey, look where you're going, idiot!'

I'm tempted to shout something back, but don't.

The sky becomes grey and it begins to rain. I hold onto turquoise railings and look out onto the sea. The sound of the waves merges with the cars driving past.

I turn my back on the sea, cross the road, and walk into a small winding alleyway packed with antique shops, jewellers and boutiques. I go into a coffee shop, buy a cup of tea and a sandwich. Take a seat.

The walls are dark red. There are large wooden coffee tables and small antique windows that only let in a small amount of light. Most of the tables are unoccupied, except for two elderly ladies who are chatting about the marriage of Prince Edward and Sophie Rhys-Jones, whilst eating scones and drinking tea.

The warmth of the room is soothing and relaxing.

I take off my watch, a birthday gift from Yvonne, and look at the engraving on the back.

To Martin, with all of my love, Yvonne.

I leave for the station.

As I put my key in the door I make a decision. I will tell her. I will tell her tonight.

The house is in darkness.

'Surprise!'

The room has been decorated with balloons, banners, fairy lights, and photographs of me as a child. The dining room table is covered with food, bottles of Champagne and presents. My friends, family, neighbours, and colleagues, are all standing in front of me, waiting for a reaction. All of this has been arranged for me.

An imposter.

Yvonne rubs my arm and passes me a drink.

'Did you know? You knew, didn't you?'

'No, really, I didn't,' I say, honestly.

Anna is back from her first term at Bristol University.

'Happy birthday, Dad!'

'Thanks. Did you know about this as well?'

She laughs.

'Are you all right? You look very thin.'

'Don't worry, I'm fine.'

'You sure? Do you need more money?'

'Stop worrying, I'm fine. Well, actually, if you're offering, there's a pair of shoes I've had my eye on.'

We smile.

Her mobile phone rings.

'Hold on Dad. Be back in a few minutes.'

I go outside for a cigarette and Jack, a friend from work, joins me.

'How about I whip your arse at a game of poker?'

'Sounds like fighting talk. Yeah, all right then.'

11:15pm

I adjust the straps of my dress and pour another glass of Champagne. The party seems to be going well. Most of the food has been eaten. That's good, I was worried that I might have made too much. Anna and her friends are dancing to a song by Steps. Martin is playing poker. I think he is enjoying himself. I hope so. He seemed strange at breakfast this morning.

Claudia approaches. She has just dyed her hair fire engine red. I'm envious.

'Yvonne, come out to the garden with me.'

'Sure, what are you up to?'

I follow her to the garden.

She opens her handbag and takes out a joint.

'What are you doing? Where did you get that?'

'I found it in Thomas' trouser pocket. When I was doing his washing.'

'Oh dear. What are you going to do? Did you speak to him?'

'What kind of a mother do you think I am? I confiscated it, of course. But, well, I thought maybe we could smoke it.'

We laugh.

'No. We shouldn't.'

'Come on, you know you want to.'

'Oh, okay, come on then.'

I've missed Claudia since she moved to the other side of the city. I remember when she used to refer to other women in the street as Stepford Wives. She would distinguish between them by using their house numbers, for example, 'Stepford Wife No 32' and 'Stepford Wife No 17'. I'd tell her not to be mean, but she knew that I would laugh every time she said it.

Claudia sits on the rusty swing and I pick up a patio chair and sit beside her. She lights the joint, inhales then passes it to me. I inhale, just a little, then pass it back.

We take a sip of wine.

'You still seeing Roger?'

'I ended it. Had a big row about his mother.'

'What happened?'

'Nothing I did seem seemed good enough for her. She criticized my cooking, my house, what I wore, even Thomas. I confronted him about it. He told me I was overreacting. Being irrational'

'What did you say to that?'

'The air was definitely blue, put it that way.'

We laugh.

'So, how are things with you?'

'I don't know. I don't know if I should say this, but-'

'What is it?'

I stare at the pond.

'I don't know. It's. Erm. Martin. He's distant.'

'Are you arguing? Or-'

'Well, not really. We don't talk. Well we talk, but we don't really talk. That doesn't even make sense.'

'Yeah, it does. Are things okay, well, you know.'

'Okay I suppose. But sometimes I wonder if there is someone else.'

'No, he wouldn't do that. He loves you.'

Claudia moves her hand, trying to rest it on my shoulder.

'Argh! Ouch!'

Claudia has fallen off the swing.

I try to help her up but she pulls me down with her. We lay on the grass for several minutes laughing, until we decide that it might be best if we went inside.

I eat the last slice of my birthday cake and look around room. All of the guests have left except for Yvonne's brother Derek and his wife, Sue. There are several half empty beer cans and glasses of wine on the table and balloons, crisps and wrapping paper on the floor.

'Hey, how about a sing song?' Derek suggests.

I stand up, walk over to the stereo and look through some of the CDs.

'What about some Irish music?'

I choose Danny Boy. We all get up and sing, trying to link arms and hold our drinks at the same time. Derek falls over onto the coffee table, almost breaking it.

'Come on, it's probably time I took you home.'

'Thanks for a great party. It's been a fab night. Happy birthday! You're old like us now!'

'Thanks.'

We walk them to the door, hug and say goodbye then sit back on the sofa. Yvonne takes a sip of her red wine and puts it on the coffee table. Her eyes are half open. She puts her head on my chest and I put my arm around her shoulders   She looks peaceful, as if she is about to fall asleep.

'Did you enjoy your party Martin?'

'Yeah, great. Thank you. I don't think I've ever seen your mum that drunk. She polished off that bottle of tequila. She was telling some filthy jokes.'

'My mum? Never!'

We both laugh.

She sits up and we are face-to-face. Her eyes struggle to focus as she looks at me. 'Martin, are we okay? You could talk to me about anything. You know that, don't you?'

'Yeah, of course. Hey, do you fancy a cocktail? Probably not a good idea but why not'

'You know you can talk to me.' Her expression has changed.

I want to tell her. Then I imagine how she would react. I stand up, walk into the kitchen and look through the drinks cupboard.

'How about a Long Island Tea?'

No answer. Yvonne is asleep on the sofa.

I put a cushion underneath her head and cover her with a blanket. I will tell her tomorrow.

Ashleigh Davies

Bolted

The words lay heavy like a scab in the mouth,
And the space between, the slender paces,
The shift of your body from mine
Chasmed into an empty grave.

Blanketed away from the shallow of my chest,
You took to the hillside;
Clinging to the brushed mane of your horse,
A grey smear, swift against the stage of green.

And amidst the hooved stomp –
A shoe thrown at a cantering swipe,
A silver cup spilling sodden clods of earth
Against the rush of cobbled mountain stones.

I stood a bristling voyeur upon your return;
Stable door ajar, the flapping exit of my tongue,
And the glistening envelope of waiting night,
The sweeping applause of the gravel road home.

About Being a Woman

Tell me about being a woman,
About where your passions swell;
How the heady trips of love hit you
Presumably with their floral accoutrements.

Tell me about how it feels
To hold your own warm, newborn flesh,
The life that was singularly a part of you,
A tight ball of elastic love to bend and not break.

Tell me about how you really feel
When your husband holds your damp-rag hand,
And the slow drip of his unkind lust
Pools into shadows at the foot of the bed.

Tell me about how you left the nest
To follow the lines in the map of your hand,
In pursuit of the rawness of the earth
The barren ground, bereft of saplings.

Tell me about your scattered seeds,
As real as dreams in that marital cave,
That forced you to wake and cradle
Your own head full of divorce.

Tell me about being a woman,
And how delivery held you still in time,
Incomplete, yet undiminished,
A woman on the cusp of the sublime.

Futures

I felt the words loop from the circle of your mouth,
The cocked bow of your upper lip framing
A dusk confessional, as we sat cross-legged,
The pale illumination of the bedside lamp
Throwing our shadow across the floor
Like the strewn clothes of our first encounter.

I remember feeling the peculiar weight
That trembled in the path of the past
That your present turned up and left disturbed,
Like the dark soil, pooled
At the foot of the garden, that had made way
For the growth of seed, our cherry tree.

The tangle of shade now dispersed
By the click of the lamp;
The soft cluck of parting lips
Trembling down to the inverted totem,
A tangle of roots and dense earth;
The organs within smarting with life.

Lepidoptery

When the shock of our love
Hit the sheets,
Somewhere in the writhing
Depths of my mind
Something was broken;
Not just splintered
Like the uneasy friendship of our youth –
Shattered, in the manner
Of your hammering pen.
                    I woke up just after midnight, starved.
You wore a scarlet ribbon
Around your slender wrist;
I took it
And deposited its frayed skein
Into the recesses of my mind,
Folding it
Into a neat butterfly of meaning,
A single unit
Of intense passion,
          And thought later,
Before you woke,
If you would mind
If I scattered it across a page –
A page now so charged
That my fingertips
Still get stung by its contents.

Letters

I didn't realise until much too late
That the faded stains on the hull of our bureau
Were letters that had failed
To make it from the safe womb of your pen
Onto the letters we exchanged like vows.

A slow dance of deep blue carnations,
Some in the form of fingerprints –
Others long and straggled stems,
Keen saplings borne of the mind,
The nature that failed them later in life.

*

There was a time when you insisted
That I was like a doctor of letters,
That I could scrape them up like scrabble pieces
And heal them through the umbilical cord
Of my arm that belonged to you, my right.

Those letters, I told you that night,
Were too far gone,
Our bureau nothing more now
Than the crude, stained sheet
That carried with it miscarriage.

And we could not cry
Because we did not know
The losses that had befallen us:
One, two, three years ago
When the letters were first conceived.

*

And so that got me thinking:
Did it take us both to conceive
The aborted letters, now nothing more
Than ink-blotch petals on old wood;
The vessel of our early hope.

Or were they your own
Curious affair;
The slow drip of conscience
That you would later wash
From your hands.

Common Ground

You left me wishing to be more
Than just the red in your rainbow,
Daubed across the naked canvas
Of your soul,
Stretched so taught that it might break
When the sweeping palette of your tongue
Lashed its words across the expanse,
And like an angry typewriter
The words got punched through to purgatory;
A horizon of shattered vowels
Amounting to little more
Than a dozen strangled noises,
The guttural throw of words left
Unsaid between our lips –
Just thirsting for a rain of ink
To hammer them into concrete shape,
So that we might have them back;
The small and discreet knot of secrets
That made you and me us.

Adam Rivers

Chilli

I place his food in front of him,
chilli.

I sit opposite,
He watches me eye up the razor scars across his wrists,
Red and fresh they scream at you in the silence.
Our eyes meet, he looks at his plate with a heavy head.
'You know that's wrong mate?'
I ask, rhetorically.
My baby brother, 19, struggling with the world.
'So many people care about you...
PAUSE
...I spoke with Dad, he's worried, you know?'
He covers his scars and sinks into his chili.
'It's not as good as Mum's, huh?'
He smiles,
'No, she cooks it properly.' He Smirks.
We laugh.

Katie-Rose Somerville

'Dream' by Salvador Dali

The air is
Sweet pomegranate,
Moist fish and fear.

Metallic, mechanic,
The rifle aims
At its prey.

Big cats pounce,
The white beauty
Is unaware.

Joints bend and crack,
Tigers gasp,
The shot loaded.

Silence.

Earlier that day

Chores to do –
Go to Tesco for milk
See Pam at number 4
Take car for M.O.T
Drop dog at Mum's house
Tidy kitchen, clean floor
Sort electricity

A fuse blown
A switch flipped

Girl found hanging from the monkey bars

Crash

Green merges with orange
Windscreen shattered
Scattered with red dots

Scrap loaded on the truck
Glass gathered, bagged
The roadside hosed
Cones picked up
Tape cut away
Cars fly down the motorway

Anni Walsh

Grave-bound Sonnet

Salt clogs up your arteries
Pasta tends to make you fat,
A hundred thousand sweeteners
Can cause cancer in a rat.
Wrap your joint in aluminium,
Years hence wonder where you're at.
Sugar gives you diabetes,
Red meat causes heart attacks.
Lungs and heart both lie in wait
For anyone who's smoking.
Decaff has carcinogens,
Caffeine stops you sleeping:
Condemned to bed and forced to lie,
Choose which way you want to die.

The Shoplifter

Lost, forlorn, alone and weary.
Neatly buttoned cardigan
And worn, old jacket,
Not enough thread left to keep out the cold.

As grey as the weekly washing
He now had to take to the laundry.
His wife had died, you see,
And he just couldn't quite manage
Without her.

That's why he took the clothes,
Which he laid out on her side of the bed.
Slowly, with shaking hands,
He took out her photograph,
Crumpled, like his face,
And stained with the tea
That she had made for forty-six years.

He already sees the world through a window of tears.
How can you think of adding bars?

Almost

I almost rang you today.
I almost said I loved you.
But you were in a hurry,
And you said you were busy.
I said some things were more important than being in a hurry,
And you said nothing then,
But that you'd ring me back.
The conversation didn't go well.
So I never rang,
And you never rang back.

Kate Clavey

Monday 5th September 1965

Worst day of my life.
    Father worked hard,
        'Only one in ten children end up here,'
            I would much rather give up my place.
Sitting in the dark chamber,
    All of us sitting behind the cold oak benches.
        Each bench was set out the same,
            Quills and ink on the top right,
                Paper on its own in the middle of a
        wooden sea, lost.
Master Evans came in,
    The smell was eternal, cheap food stewing
        Whether it was cake or fish, it all tasted the same,
        Cold and soggy.
I gazed out of the window into sunshine,
    Where I longed to be a flower, dancing in the field, to be free–
    THUD!
        'I must always pay attention'
            Etched into my brain,
                Leave that prison behind,
Parents remind me
    'Only one in ten.'

Danica Green

Chasing Rainbows

A life spent chasing the rain,
Following rainbows that always escape
Over impassable hills
Or hidden in dense wood, and I,
Desperate to once run fingers through their yielding light
Fruit juice fingertips to paint with
When the storm has passed by.

I found a wayward tail,
Only once, in clear winter skies
I stumbled on its resting place,
Deep to its eyes in lake water
Calling to me,
Beckoning with seven-fingered hands,
Here lies wealth, gold coins for the boatman.
You need do aught but drown.

Womb Thorns

Romantic declinations,
My husband never gives me real flowers,
Plastic stems and cheap petals
Litter my pillow,
Breakfast tray with red-dressed eggs,
Green leaf floating in the orange juice.

I never asked why, but still he told me,
It is not expense or longevity,
Only principal.

I should be the one to give him life.

Friend

Braced up against the window frame,
Hard eyes, hard hands
Watching ghosts of the neighbourhood
Dancing in the streets
Next to the rusted Ford
Front yard couch
Jungle.

Gauzy lace of the drapes in eyes,
Burn, tickle, twitch, dried retinas,
Glass inch cage in ancient wood,
Holding cell for those uninvited,
Stadium of the perpetual voyeur,
Silent watcher of long celebrations.

Eyes twinkle, flick to the watcher's den,
Mocking glance
Tender judge
Will you come out and play tonight?
Silent refusal
Withdrawal
Back to the door listening to their sounds.

My, That's Unfortunate

I once read about a scientist who died from bubonic plague.
He was studying it in a lab,
A supposedly safe variety of the bacteria,
Modified so it couldn't live off the iron in a person's body,
Which is what the plague does.
It turns out this scientist had a rare medical condition,
That he didn't know about,
Where he had a lot more iron in his body than people normally do,
So the bacteria took hold.
It's like they took the teeth and claws out of a lion,
But the prey smelled so deliciously meaty,
The lion said 'fuck it' and gummed him to death.

Contributors

Anthony Cerrato is a 20 year old student from Llandudno Junction, North Wales, currently studying English and Creative Writing at U.W.I.C. His interests include reading, painting, playing guitar and skateboarding. More of his work can be found at http://anthonycerrato.blogspot.com

Kate Clavey is currently studying English and Creative Writing at the University of Wales Institute, Cardiff. Her writing has previously been published in *Great Minds United in Poetry* Vol III and *T.A.L.E.S From Wales* Vol 1 and hopes to continue to make the most of the opportunities available in Cardiff.

Ashleigh Davies was born in Abergavenny in 1990 and grew up in the surrounding area, the landscape and society of which strongly influences his writing. Currently studying English and Creative Writing at the University of Wales Institute, Cardiff, his literary influences include Owen Sheers, Adam Foulds and Ted Hughes.

Ellen Duncan was born in Swansea to a Scottish father and English mother. She is currently studying English and Creative Writing at UWIC. In her spare time she enjoys horse riding, reading and listening to music, with an ever-expanding iTunes library, but never enough space for her books.

Danica Green is a fledgling writer who has recently graduated from university and currently spends most of her time wandering around Wales looking confused.

Sam Harman is a native of Saundersfoot, residing in Cardiff and currently studying English & Creative Writing at UWIC (and writing about himself in third-person). He also attempts to make music in his spare time.

Sophie Harris is nineteen years old and currently studying English and Creative Writing at UWIC to obtain the necessary qualifications to teach English in a number of countries across Europe. She is mainly interested in writing fiction based on revolution, crime, fantasy or the supernatural.

Andrew Henderson lives and studies in Cardiff, though he was born in Swansea (don't tell the locals). As a consequence of recently kicking his smoking habit he now rages quite a bit and uses the C word quite a lot.

Kate Herbert has just completed and MA in Creative Writing and English at UWIC. She has written features for National papers including *The Independent*, *The Mail on Sunday* and *The New York Times*. Her articles and interviews have appeared in *She*, *Cosmopolitan* and *Marie Claire*. She spent three years as a Writers' Agent in Covent Garden, syndicating her own and other writers' work. More recently she has worked as a CPPD tutor for UWIC, specialising in creative writing and art therapy.

Matthew Herman is a recent graduate of UWIC's English and Creative Writing BA (hons). He is about to take off on a single flight to work in Montreal for an advertising company, writing television commercials. His reading interests include Stephen King and Bret Easton Elis.

Barry Hogan is a postgraduate English & Creative Writing student at UWIC. Originally from Royston (Herts), he has lived in Cardiff Since 2001. 'A Return to Brighton' is his first piece of published writing and is inspired by the time he was a student in the city in the mid-nineties. Dedicated to Phil.

Catherine Hoyle is a Welsh writer from Saint Athan. Catherine completed her degree at UWIC in English and Creative Writing (BA) in 2011; through her characters' actions, she explores the poignancy of memory and the nature of the human condition within her work.

Emma Hutson is the person in the dented fiesta on the M4 between Gloucester and Cardiff who is singing so emphatically that you slow down in the middle-lane just to watch her for a moment. She also studies English and writes a bit.

A. Owen James has tried his very best to steer away from writing anything of merit whilst studying Creative Writing at Cardiff's UWIC. He is an uninteresting human and an appalling writer. His work should be burned before being forgotten. His pens should be broken and his fingers snapped.

Liam Johnson received second prize and the audience vote for 'verbal pyrotechnics' at Academi's John Tripp Award for Spoken Poetry in 2009, and has since performed at venues across Wales and spilling into England. This is his first piece of published fiction.

Ben Jones was born in Bangor, North Wales and currently lives just down the coast in Penmaenmawr. He has always loved to read and whenever the opportunity to write a story arose in school he'd take it straight away. He has just finished an English and Creative Writing degree at UWIC, Cardiff.

Andrew Paul Lambert completed a BA (hons) Modern History and English degree at UWIC in 2011, where he has currently enrolled to undertake an MA in English and Creative Writing. Andrew lives in Cwmbran with his wife Liz and their two children, Charlie and Evie.

Jane Levy is a senior lecturer at UWIC's Cardiff School of Management who has a passion for English Literature. These stories are some of her first as a creative writer and focus on the complex experience of being a woman. 'Two Women, One Day' is dedicated to Anastacia.

Katy Lewis is originally from Pontypridd and lives and works in Cardiff. She is also studying at the University towards an MA in English and Creative Writing. Following completion she aims to continue with her re-ignited passion for writing.

Jennifer Lindley lives in Cornwall, has a degree in English and Popular Culture from UWIC and is currently studying for her Masters in English and Creative writing.

Charis Lippett is an English and Creative Writing student at UWIC with a chronic dependency on tea and Twitter. When she's not writing for coursework, she co-edits and contributes to www.creulife.com, a Canadian website starting 'a conversation on creativity and life'.

Rachel Shepherd is a Cornish writer currently studying English and Creative Writing at University of Wales Institute, Cardiff. She also sings and writes lyrics with The Word Virus Essay found on www.myspace.com.thewordvirusessay.

Adam Rivers is currently an undergraduate student of English Literature and Creative Writing at UWIC.

Katie-Rose Somerville is currently reading for a BA Educational Studies and English. She is a youth worker in the local community and she enjoys interacting with a diverse range of people. She hopes to work within an environment that encompasses her interests in people, literature and society.

Stacey Taylor has previously had a short story appear on the website of publishing company Headline and was one of five finalists in the Miss Write competition run by Little, Brown, Waterstone's and *Cosmopolitan* which received over 3000 entries. She is currently working on a novel aimed at teenage girls.

Sally Thomas is a thirty six year old mature student currently studying an undergraduate BA honours degree in English and Creative Writing. She was born in Cardiff and has lived here most of her life. She currently resides in the north of the city with her husband and three young children.

Alex Trew is currently an undergraduate student of English and Creative Writing at UWIC. When he isn't writing he spends his time learning French and pretending to look for a job.

Siobhan Tumelty is a twenty-four year old Waitress from Cardiff who makes 'skinny' lattes with full fat milk if you don't say please and thank you. She writes some of the time, sings all of the time and has on more than one occasion been said to resemble Jack Nicholson.

Anni Walsh is a recently retired personal injury and criminal lawyer, married and now working as a milliner in Cardiff. Anni has always been interested in writing and is in the process of writing a novel for which she has received useful support and assistance from the novel-writing class at UWIC

Sonnie Hazell Wills, between bouts of mania, spends her time writing stories and poetry, drinking cans of coke and meticulously separating her recycling. She lived with beautiful people and her goldfish, Dr Speedy, Slasher, Hades and Fluffy, until they all died. The fish, not the people.

L. Windridge has a degree in English Literature and Drama from Manchester University and a Postgraduate Diploma in Dramatherapy. She has enjoyed synthesising her life experiences creatively on the masters in English and Creative Writing at UWIC.

Tamara Winkler is the Business Support Manager for the Cardiff School of Education in UWIC. She is also studying for a PhD in Perceptions of Strategic Change. She has been writing for many years with a focus on short stories, poetry and children's stories.